# Hawai'i

# The Best Day Hikes on the Big Island!

## Robert Frutos

One of Hawai'i's best known
Nature Photographers & Camera Artist's

Text by Robert Frutos

ISBN-13: 978-1502732583    ePub ISBN-10: 1502732580

**Also by Robert Frutos;**

Day Hikes in Hawai'i Volcanoes National Park: The Best Places to See the Unusual, Find the Unexpected, and Experience the Magnificent!

A Photographer's Guide to the Big Island: Being in the Right Place, at the Right time, for the Best Image!

A Photographer's Guide to Hawai'i Volcanoes National Park: Being in the Right Place, at the Right time, for the Best Image!

Hawai'i  The most Beautiful Places to Visit on the Big Island

*See full list of book titles by Robert Frutos on Page 140/141*

**www.hawaiiphototours.org**

**www.hawaiisacredsitestours.com**

**www.robertfrutos.com**

**email: rfphoto3@gmail.com    Phone: 808 345 – 7179**

# Dedication

To those who seek the beauty of nature,
and know how to listen inwardly,

&

and for those who gain inspiration
by being in Her presence!

## Rainforest Trail
### Hawai'i Volcanos National Park

All Images by Robert Frutos

# Table of Context

# Preface

**Hawai'i is truly one of the planet's most fascinating natural wonders -** with pristine beaches, warm tropical breezes, turquoise waters, gently swaying palms, magnificent waterfalls, endless rainbows and an active volcano. Hawai'i offers a unique and unforgettable experience.

While all the Hawaiian Islands have their own unique beauty and stunning vistas, with cultural hues and flavors, the Big Island of Hawai'i retains its own remarkable wealth of unique, unexpected, and magnificent features.

Through time, the Big Island has developed its own multi-colored flora and fauna. Its own distinctive and unusual evolution of life… with unceasing lava flows, vast bio-diverse forests, and a nearly 14,000 ft. high mountain. It also has it own endemic species of birds, insects, and sea life.

The Big Island of Hawai'i contains one the worlds greatest concentrations of climate types. From dry, coastal, desert strand to some of the wettest spots on earth, from warm humid tropical lushness to stark, barren, snow - capped mountains, the Big Island offers an astonishing array of great beauty and wonder.

Perhaps, because it is the biggest island in the state of Hawai'i that vast tracts of open land remain virtually untouched and accessible (all the other islands put together fit into its footprint.)

It is for these reasons that I choose to make the Big Island my home. And because I am foremost a camera artist/nature photographer, I have spent untold hours, days, months and years - exploring and discovering the many unique features and diverse areas of the Big Island, including the little-known, rarely visited, remote locations, as well as the more easily accessible sites.

There is so much beauty and wonder to be found here… from **Hawai'i Volcanoes National Park's** surreal lavascapes, its spectacular pluming Halema'uma'u Crater, and spewing steam vents, to the wild Puna and Ka'ū Coast.

From 14,000 ft. Mauna Kea, to the white sand beaches in the Kona and Kohala district, and to the rainforests and waterfalls, there is so much to see and experience.

**This guidebook will help YOU access these special places, that you may find them in comfort and with ease. You will not have to guess what they look like, or how long it takes to get there, or how to get there.**

**The details and particulars are all right here in this guidebook, ready to orient you and send you on your merry way!**

**You will find that the Big Island of Hawai'i is such a Fabulous Place...** not only for the extraordinary beauty and magnificence of the sweeping views and tropical panoramas, but for the phenomenal spirit that pervades the native culture, and the traditions that keep them thriving.

A spirit known as the Aloha Spirit is felt, both in the love and liveliness of its people, AND as a *living breathing vitality* that permeates the landscape.

It is for the above reasons that the Big Island offers both excellent and unique day hikes. From the easy, to the moderate, each filled with a splendor and wonderment all of their own.

**And it's all here just waiting for you!**

# Introduction

## This Book Is For *YOU!*

Most people come to the Big Island with less time than they would like. WITH SO MANY POSSIBILITIES AND OPTIONS, many find themselves unable to easily locate the excellent places they would like to experience while visiting here.

Whether you are only here for only a couple of days, or have the luxury of a longer stay -
*this guidebook will prove to be invaluable, as it shares the best and most beautiful day hikes on the Big Island and how to easily access them.*

*This book will save you precious time and effort.*

*You don't have to scout out and discover the best day hikes and you don't have to wonder if you missed any of the great or spectacular places.*

**Rather you can casually move from one marvelous landscape/seascape to another, with clear expectation and relaxed certainty, given the amount of time you do have available.**

To be sure, scouting out and discovering the best places are part of the fun while visiting any new locale, *but if you are short on time, why not put the odds in your favor?*

Moreover, Hawai'i The Best Day Hikes on the Big Island, shares information about each place listed: Where it is, what to expect, and when the best time to visit is. It informs as to whether you may need extra layers… should you go visit the Mauna Kea Summit, or Hawai'i Volcanoes National Park for example. It also offers safety tips, towards assuring an incident free visit.

**If you are here, for one or many fun-filled adventures, full of the wondrous, the beautiful and the magnificent, then Hawai'i: The Best Day Hikes on the Big Island is the book for you!**

*May you enjoy and appreciate Hawai'i's s great wonder and beauty.*

# Let the Adventure Begin…

For the ease of finding the best day hikes on Hawai'i Island – let us begin in Kona, where the vast majority of people arrive on the Big Island.

The highway system on the Big Island is very simplistic. Highway 19 runs both north and south from the Kona airport, and is found with great ease.

Going south from the airport about 7 miles, where Highway 19 reaches Palani Street in Kona, it becomes Highway 11 - continuing as Highway 11 all the way to Hilo. In Hilo, it changes back to Highway 19 - continuing as Highway 19 all the way back to Kona.

It is the same road, the same highway, it just changes numbers in Kona and back again in Hilo. This is the main highway that circles the entire island.

**With one exception** (see below*) we will begin by going directly north from Kona and circling the island through Hilo – then returning via South Point, and once again back to Kona, all with a number of impressive side routes to plenty of trails along the way.

The day hikes will be most easily found by locating the specific highway mile markers for each trail. The distance and time from Kona and/or Hilo is also included.

Most of the day hikes can easily be done in one day, sometimes numerous hikes can be done in a day, depending on when you start and how you plan the day. In some cases, sunrise and sunset will enhance the setting, in other cases sunrise and sunset light are not a particularly strong factor.

*To help you best optimize your time, a "**best time to be there**" paragraph, or two is included, for every location.*

Certainly follow your heart and give yourself permission to have the best experience possible. And if you focus on quality over quantity you will allow yourself the opportunity to have a very rich, perhaps even an extraordinary experience.

Most day hikes and/or trailheads will have safe, easy access. A few sites require more effort, as they are more remote.

**\* The one exception will be our first stop… Pu'uhonua o Honaunau (The Place of Refuge) which is to the south of Kona.**

It is an excellent place to begin your experience, as visiting Pu'uhonua o Honaunau allows you to experience classic Hawai'i… gently swaying palms, coastal scenics, ki'i (wooden carved figures) Hawaiian green sea turtles, incredible waves, and outstanding sunsets.

Pu'uhonua o Honaunau has a tangible atmosphere of radiant peace and tranquility, and once served as a significant place of refuge (see page 19.)

However long you may visit the Big Island, whether for a couple of days or over several weeks, drink deeply of its beauty, its wonder, and magnificence, *and especially* allow yourself to bask fully in the Spirit of Aloha!

# A Quick Word ... About What to Bring, Awareness & Safety!

While visiting these beautiful locations, for your over-all convenience, it is often best to have a hat, cap, or visor, for either sun or rain. It is also an excellent idea to have sunscreen, just in case, because the sun can be intense in places. Sunglasses are optional.

Regarding footwear, sandals or slippa's as they are called here, work well in most places. However, be aware, it may be best to protect your feet at times (from lava - scratches and cuts) by wearing comfortable walking/hiking shoes.

Food and water are available in most areas around the island, *but it is wise* to carry food or snacks and always have water with you, out on the trail.

It is best to have extra food in the car as well, in case you stay out late and the restaurants are closed by the time you return. Hawai'i does close up early compared to mainland services

Shorts and a t-shirt or a light blouse are often the norm for day hikes. The weather, however, is un-predictable and can change at any given moment, so best to carry layers with you and be prepared.

If you go to Hawai'i Volcanoes National Park, it can be quite cool there in the evenings. Thanks to its higher elevation – 4000 ft. and the windward (rainier) location of the park, it is always cooler than most of the rest of the island.

At least in the upper elevations of the park, so it best to

bring a sweater or light jacket. Moreover, it's always wise to have rain gear and a fleece on hand, especially in winter.

## Awareness & Respect!

**Please respect the beautiful places you visit during your hikes and travel.** To show respect... simply follow your common sense: don't disturb the environment, don't harm plants or rocks, or other natural and/or prominent features, and do not leave trash.

By leaving the environment, as we have found it, or perhaps even better than we found it (by picking up trash, if there is any) we ensure that these trails and locations remain both beautiful and accessible for generations to come.

As the well worn adage goes:
Take only pictures, leave only footprints!

## Safety Tips!

Commons sense is the key word for having a safe and pleasurable visit while on the Big Island.

Drink plenty of water, so as to not get dehydrated, wearing clothing and footwear appropriate to your location, and being aware of that unsuspecting rouge wave that comes along every so often, will be a big step towards assuring an incident free visit.

Also the Big Island has no four lane freeways, only two lane highways, and the top speed limit is still only 55 m.p.h. - so be aware and be alert - while driving the islands highways and roadways.
**Remember always, Safety First!**

# Expect the Unexpected...

The geographical location and positioning of the Big Island of Hawai'i affords more unexpected natural events, occurring more often, than on the US mainland.

Mists, rain, rainbows, cloudbursts, God rays, white rainbows, and moonbows (just like a rainbow, except at night, created around a full moon) are all abundant here.

Other natural occurrences include: the wind, and the moon - in any phase. And of course, one hour around either sun rise and sun set, also known as the "magic hour."

While the daily events in the third paragraph can be more or less calculated, the natural events in the second paragraph can appear unexpectedly and at any moment. They may last from a few seconds to several minutes.

Being aware of, and on the look out for such occurrences, will help give more wonder, more beauty to your day, *and* allow for a more magical over-all experience.

Ki'i, Pu'uhonua o Honaunau

# First Stop…
# Pu'uhonua o Honaunau
## (The Place of Refuge)

Pu'uhonua o Honaunau is an ideal place to begin, as it allows you to experience a classic Hawai'i… gently swaying palms, coastal scenics, ki'i (wooden carved figures) Hawaiian green sea turtles, incredible waves, and outstanding sunsets.

Pu'uhonua o Honaunau has an atmosphere of radiant peace and tranquility that matches its beauty, and it once served as a significant place of refuge (for full details, be sure to pick up their brochure once there.)

While there is an "official" trail that will lead you to Ki'ilae, an old Hawaiian village, and the hike is well worth it, the experience of classic Hawai'i can be found simply by hiking and exploring the area.

**One exploration…** is to make your way to the visitor center at the end of the parking lot. Facing the visitor center, turn right and walk through the sheltered walkway. At the end of the walkway, continue straight until you reach a stonewall.

From the stonewall you will observe the Hale o Keawe – a temple and mausoleum surrounded by several ki'i (sacred wooden images.)

Make your way round Keone'ele cove to Hale o Keawe - keep an eye out for Hawaiian green sea turtles (Honu) swimming in the bay, or resting on the shore.

Continuing past Hale o Keawe, the trail proceeds beyond it and then passes the 'Āle'ale'a Heiau, an ancient heiau (Hawaiian Outdoor Temple) used for relaxing and hula, and continues towards the palm trees in the short distance.

At the apex of the trail just before it loops back towards the great wall, if you observe closely you will notice an unmarked faint trail heading directly towards the palm trees. Take this trail, it will lead you through the palm trees and beyond.

Now you have come to a bit of white sand and a lava bench. Make your way gently and diagonally to the right, as you walk towards the edge of the sea.

Your destination is to reach the farthest point from the Pu'uhonua o Honaunau compound. There you will find two seawater pools. This is an exhilarating place to stand and watch the waves come splashing in, or to observe the quiet serenity of a magnificent sunset.

**Another exploration would be...** to walk in on the gravelly/dirt road also located at the end of the visitor center parking lot - but to the left as you face the visitor center.

As you begin to walk on the gravel road, in a short distance you will see a sign for the trail to Ki'ilae village on the left, also known as the 1871 Trail.

From the junction of this trail, you can either follow the trail, or continue on the road to the picnic area.

If you follow the 1871 Trail, you will be led through an area rich in Hawaiian history and natural resources. The trail is about one mile and flat, but it is a moderately strenuous hike through rough lava.

Please wear sturdy shoes, a hat, sunscreen and carry

plenty of water. And please stop by the visitor center to pick up an informative trail guide specific to this trail (you have to ask for it.)

Stay on the trail until you reach the abandoned village of Ki'ilae. Definitely worth the hike, and there is a great panoramic view of the coastline just past the Alahaka Ramp and the (now closed) Waiu-o-Hina Lava Tube entrance.

If you continue on the road by the picnic tables you will see picturesque palm trees, and lovely coastal views and oceans hues, as well as excellent waves.

If you go to the end of the picnic area parking lot you find a coastal trail that will connect you to the Ki'ilae village trail.

So either way you decide to go, you can make this a loop trail by starting out on the Ki'ilae village trail, then looping back along the clearly marked coast trail (which is about half way back from Ki'ilae village.) This will bring you to the picnic area and you can continue on the road until you reach the visitor center.

Or, by staying on the road, and catching the coastal trail, at the far end of the picnic area parking lot. The coastal trail leads to the Ki'ilae village trail and then you can return back to the visitor center.

Either way you decide to go, there will be much to see, and much to engage you in wonder.

## Exploring the Alahaka Ramp

Pu'uhonua O Honaunau National Historical Park

## Enjoying the Sunset
## Pu'uhonua O Honaunau National Historical Park

*The best time to be there: From Pu'uhonua O Honaunau you will be able to see some amazing sunsets. Towards early evening the larger crowds have moved on, thus allowing you a more quiet and reflective experience. Otherwise, being there any time of day is a real wonder and joy.*

## How to get to Pu'uhonua O Honaunau National Historical Park

Pu'uhonua O Honaunau National Historical Park is located about 22 miles south of Kailua-Kona off of Highway 11.

Head south on Highway 11 until you reach clearly marked Highway 160, just past mile marker 104. Go 4 miles down Highway 160 from Highway 11 and you will see an obvious sign for Pu'uhonua O Honaunau.

Turn left at the sign and go down about a block, it is very easy to locate. There you find a kiosk and there is park entrance fee of $5.00 per vehicle. The entrance fee is good for 7 days. (and includes entrance into Hawai'i Volcanoes National Park for 7 days as well.)

Park operating hours: Park opens at 7 AM. Park closes at sunset. For current park info., please call the visitor center at (808) 328-2326 ext 1702

The Visitor Center is open 8:30 AM - 4:30 PM daily.

Distance from Kona: Approximately 22 miles
Time from Kona: 30 – 40 minutes, depending on traffic.

# Kaloko-Honokohau
# National Historic Park

Heading north of Kona, we come to the Kaloko-Honokohau National Historic Park. There are a number of trails choices here, but the one you are seeking is the coastal hike known as the Ala Hele Kahakai Trail.

Part of a much longer trail, this section of the trail follows the pristine coastline for about a mile and a quarter, or a mile and a half, depending on how far you choose to hike it.

Once in the parking lot (see directions on how to get there below) and facing the ocean - there will be the large Kaloko fishpond to your right. Again while facing the ocean - the trail begins to the far left, after the small picnic area. It's easy to find.

As you begin your hike, you may notice a subtle change, as though you are stepping back into a sense of timelessness. This can happen due to the sound of the gentle lapping waves mixed with the feeling of deep relaxation from the warm sun.

It can also happen because Kaloko-Honokohau National Historical Park is the site of an ancient Hawaiian settlement. And what you feel/sense can be a part of the energy that has been created by its early inhabitants – an energy of peace, wonder, and appreciation.

The first part of the trail is through a combination of shrubs and trees, with the constant melody of birdsong and the sound of the sea off to your right.

About a third of the way into the hike you will notice the first of three trails heading off to the left. This one is known as the Ala Hele Hu'e Hu'e trail, and was once part of a major path way towards and into the cooler, upper elevations. Today it will take you across a massive lava field and only back to the highway.

Continuing on the Ala Hele Kahakai Trail, the trail becomes part of the shoreline itself. You may notice ancient Hawaiian fishing traps and fish ponds. The fish traps and fish ponds in this locale are some of the best examples of Hawaiian stone work acuity – each a marvel of ingenuity.

You may also come across local wildlife including honu (Hawaiian green sea turtles), native birds, and occasionally even a Hawaiian monk seal, sunning on the shore.

If you walk far enough you will come to a canoe house, (a thatched grass roof hut) that once protected far ranging sea-faring canoes, as well as local fishing canoes - it can't be missed.

A ways before the canoe house you will notice a second trail going off to your left. If you need a restroom, follow this trail a short bit and there you will find one.

If you continue on the trail with the restrooms, this is known as the Ala Hele Ike Hawai'i Trail, and you will end up at the visitor center.

If you continue towards the canoe house, you will see a third trail off to the left. This trail takes you to yet another park entrance.

**Honu ( Hawaiian Green Sea Turtle) at Sunset**
**Kaloko-Honokohau National Historical Park**

Near and around the canoe house there are often honu in the area. And if you go just a bit beyond the canoe house and through a break in the trees and vegetation - you will find another restroom.

Be sure to pick up the Kaloko-Honokohau brochure at the visitor center, it has a clear map of the park, and will prove very helpful. And while you are there - check with the visitor center to learn about any special programs and/or guided tours.

*The best time to be there: From Kaloko-Honokohau National Historical Park you will be able to see some astonishing sunsets. Early morning or late afternoon the larger crowds have moved on, thus allowing you a more quiet and enjoyable experience. Otherwise, being there any time of day can be an amazing experience.*

## How to get to
## Kaloko-Honokohau National Historical Park

There are three different approaches in which to enter the park. Choose according to what you want to experience and see.

1. Hale Ho'okipa (Welcome House) - **this entrance is the easiest to find, and includes the main visitor center** for the park, as well as the main parking area.

On Hwy. 19, the Queen Ka'ahumanu Highway, coming from either direction, turn makai (toward the sea) just south of the 97 m(ile) m(arker) at the signed entrance to the National Historical Park.

You'll see a circular parking area and a few structures just off the highway. The visitor center is open from 8:30 am to 4:00 pm every day, otherwise the gate is locked.

There are park rangers available to answer questions, with information and maps, water, and restrooms. This is also where the Ala Hele Ike Hawai'i trai begins into the park.

## 2. Kaloko Road – **This is the road you want to get you to the trailhead of the coastal Ala Hele Kahakai Trail - The trail described in this chapter.**

This is a rough, unpaved road that leads to Kaloko fishpond. Any passenger car will make it fine and safe, just drive slow.

Find the turnoff just north of the visitor center. There is a gate that is unlocked from 8:30 am to 5:00 pm every day.

## 3. Honokōhau Harbor - This harbor is used for small boats and several commercial diving and fishing businesses. Just south of the visitor center, find Kealakehe Parkway at a traffic light and turn makai (toward the sea).

Take the first right along the parkway and follow this road until you see the Kona Sailing Club. Park in the gravel parking lot across from a gate (just a signed opening actually, there is no gate.) You can easily see the opening and the trail from the parking lot. There are restrooms further along the trail near the shore, but not at the trailhead itself.

Distance from Kona: Approximately 3 miles
Time from Kona: 5 – 10 minutes, depending on traffic.

# Kekaha Kai State Park/
## Mahai'ula Beach & Makalawena Beach

One of the most beautiful locations to visit on the west side of the island is known locally as Makalawena Beach (pronounced mac-ah-la-va-na.) Some say it is the most beautiful beach on the island.

It has a gorgeous white sand beach and beautiful blue waters. It is very idyllic with long curving stretches of beach. And if you get there early in the day or late in the afternoon on a weekday - you will find very few people, and/or possible have it all to yourself.

It is only for the real adventurous, and because it is a bit detailed to get there, most of this description will be on how to do so and the perimeters involved (see below.)

*The best time to be there: Because this excellent beach is becoming more and more known, it can be somewhat busy at times, though not fully crowded like some of the other white sand beaches north of Kona, as it does take a bit of effort to get there. The best time, therefore, is to be there midweek, early morning or late afternoon. It's also a great place to watch the sunset or the moonrise.*

*However, please be aware that if you come in through Kehaka Kai State Park, they do not open the gate until 9 am and then the gate is locked at 7 pm.*

*So you will need to give yourself plenty of time to hike back to your car and drive back up to the highway, before they lock the gate, or you will be locked in for the night.*

*(This has happened to a couple of friends of mine and you wouldn't want to find yourself in this position.)*

*The best months for watching the sunset and the moon rise from Makalawena Beach are November, December and January, as the sun sets early, and you will have enough time to easily get back to the highway before the gate is locked.*

## How to get to **Kekaha Kai State Park/ Makalawena Beach**

Get on Highway 19 heading north from Kona. You will pass the Kona airport, continue on until you reach mile marker 91. You will soon notice a sign for **Kekaha Kai State Park**. The turn off is the next *paved* road on the left.

The pavement however, only goes a short distance to the gate. The road then becomes very bumpy. How bumpy will depend on when it was last graded. If you are in a standard car rental - drive very slowly and carefully.

If you do not feel comfortable driving on this road, park on the highway side of the gate and hike in. It's about 1.5 miles down to the sea, though it definitely seems longer.

As you near the ocean, you will see a number of cars parked along the roadway. This is where you want to park. Once parked, locate an old lava road with a chain across it, on the north side of the road (the opposite direction from Kona) right next to the parking area.

If you do not park here and continue forth another 1/8 of a mile you will arrive at **Kekaha Kai State Park** proper. The park has restrooms and picnic tables and is a nice place to relax and explore. However, the best experience begins at the chain across the lava road

From the chain across the lava road, the way is apparent. There are usually people walking to and fro. Hike along the lava road until you reach a old deserted house.

In this area you will view lovely Mahai'ula beach. A beautiful crescent shaped white sand beach. If you go no further, visiting this beach would have been worth the adventure.

However, continuing on to Makalewena beach… just past the deserted house is a trail. Continue on the trail around the crescent of the bay, until you reach an obvious coconut trees grove.

**Pristine & Serene Makalewena Beach**

Right before the coconut trees and to the right - is the trail that will get you to Makalewena beach. It crosses a barren lava field, and then all of a sudden you will find yourself walking on sand surrounded by trees and vegetation. Continue on until you reach the shore.

**On the Trail to Makalewena Beach**

Once at the shore, walk north (the opposite direction from Kona) until you reach a lava arm that stretches into the sea, just past the lava arm is the nicest beach in the area. Enjoy!

The bounce in will take about 10 to 20 minutes, depending on how fast you drive the road. And then another 15 - 20 minutes to Makalewena beach, depending on how fast you hike.

It is very dry in these parts, and usually hot, especially when hiking. Please wear sturdy shoes, a hat, sunscreen and carry plenty of water.

Distance from Kona: Approximately 9 miles
Time from Kona: 10 – 15 minutes, depending on traffic.

## There is Another Way...

There is another way to get to Makalewena beach. It is most definitely a 4-wheel drive road, but even with the best of 4-wheel drives (especially if rented) I would not recommend driving it. It is the worst 4-wheel drive road on the island, and to the inexperienced, it can reek havoc and cause damage to your vehicle.

## However you can hike in.
Going north on Highway 19 from Kona, you will pass the Kona airport, continue on until you reach mile marker 89. Midway between mm 89 and mm 88 there is a dirt road off to the left (ocean side) that is your starting destination and is fairly easy to locate.

If you come to the West Hawai'i Veterans Cemetery sign, you've gone far. Simply turn around and drive back about a half of mile. You will most likely see other cars parked near the dirt road.

Start hiking this road toward the ocean, stay on it until

you come to the first and very obvious left hand turn (near the base of Pu'u Kuili, a cinder hill.)

Turn left here and continue walking, soon you will see what I mean by being the worst 4-wheel drive on the island. Continue on until you reach the sea.

Follow the coastline (back towards Kona.) You will be walking directly along the coast through assorted (unofficial) very primitive campsites.

Hike along the coast until you come to a gate. Make your way through the ironwood forest, around the first small bay, over a lava arm, and there you are, right at the beach where you would be if you walked the other described route.

This hike will take about 45 minutes to an hour depending upon your rate of speed. As mentioned above, it is very dry in these parts, and usually hot, especially when hiking. Please wear sturdy shoes, a hat, sunscreen and carry plenty of water.

Distance from Kona: Approximately 11.5 miles
Time from Kona: approx. 15 minutes, depending on traffic.

## Other Considerations

Of the two routes, the first, via Kekaha Kai State Park is the more picturesque and enjoyable hike.

The advantage to walking in via the 4-wheel drive road is that you *are* hiking in, right from the start, and not bouncing in, nor causing any potential damage to your vehicle. You are also not time restricted by having to be back before the gate is locked at 7 pm, so you are free to get back to the highway and your car at any time.

You could make quite a day out of this adventure by hiking in on the 4-wheel drive road early in the day, then staying all day at Makalewena beach (don't forget a lunch) then watching the sunset and the moon rise, and then walking out on a full moon (don't forget a flashlight, just in case.)

Of course you could do the same via Kekaha Kai State Park. Park your car on the highway side of the gate, then hike in, following the earlier description, but it is a lot further hike back to the highway at days end, at least that's the way it feels.

Honu ( Hawaiian Green Sea Turtle)

Kiholo Bay

# Kiholo Bay

Kiholo Bay is a fabulous area, with indescribable blue waters, abundant sea turtles, and refreshingly cold water springs that bubble up and mix with the sea water.

This is a unique area, well worth the time and effort it takes to get there. It involves a bit of a hike, not strenuous, just often very warm/hot.

The major part of the hike is on an old road through Keawe trees. Keawe trees have huge thorns on them that eventually fall to the ground, so wear sturdy shoes, or, at least be on the lookout for them. If a thorn penetrates your footwear, ouch! You will most certainly know it!

When you reach the sea you begin to see why the hike was worth it!

***The best time to be there:*** *This is one of those places, that proves to be an excellent place to be any time of day. It is generally not crowded due to the effort of hiking in.*

*There are some small lava arms that project into the water of the bay. After the warm walk, this is a great place to jump in the water for a cool refreshing dip. You could also catch an excellent sunset here, but be sure and have a flashlight for the walk back to your car.*

## How to get to Kiholo Bay

On Highway 19 heading north from Kona, continue on until you reach mile marker 82. Just south of mile marker 81 is a pull over area on the makai (ocean) side of the highway.

At the pullout is a parking area just below the road. However, it is best to park on the highway, as it can be difficult getting back onto the highway in a standard rental car from the parking lot, due to loose gravel.

From the parking lot area (to the left while facing the ocean) you will find a trail that becomes an old gravel/dirt road and heads straight down to the coast.

Stay on the trail/road, as you near the coast, it will eventually curve to the left. Continue a bit further until you reach the "public access" path on your right.

Once on the sand, facing the ocean, turn right and follow the coastline back around the point to where it comes to a short wooden bridge. This is a man-made channel that allows sea turtles access to a nearby private lagoon. You can often see them here swimming to the lagoon or back toward the bay.

Continue on past the wooden bridge and soon it goes from sand to lava. Continue on the lava trail.

In about two blocks distance, if you stay next to the water, you will see a very small beach. If you follow the coastline you will come to some nice lava arms extending into the water that allow you to jump in the bay with ease.

You can also explore further by scrambling across the lava around the bay, or making your way across the bay onto the peninsula area. You should see Hawaiian green sea turtles aplenty

Distance from Kona: Approximately 18 miles
Time from Kona: approx. 25 minutes

# 'Anaeho'omalu Bay
## (known locally as "A" Bay)

This is an exceptionally picturesque area. What makes it so are the many palm trees, the plumeria bushes/trees, (and sea turtles which can be seen at the oceans edge.)

A great view around sunset is from the resort side of the huge fishponds facing the ocean. When there is no wind, you will see mirrored images, and when there is wind, the color reflections can be a sheer delight.

As for the trail, once parked, continue walking on the road (see below) past the restrooms to the coastline. For those wanting a view a sunset with sunset colors reflected in the fishpond, there is a path off to the right, just past the restrooms that will wind you around the backside of the fishpond.

**Another Glorious Sunset at A Bay**

The trail you are looking for begins right at the shoreline, and goes both north and south. This is part of the Ala Hele Kahakai Trail that begins 10 miles north at Spencer beach and continues 16 miles to the south as far as the Kona airport.

Though the trail is not visually evident in either direction at this point, as you continue to walk it will become fully apparent. If you go south (towards Kona) the trail continues directly along the coast. Many sea turtles frequent this area.

The farther south you go the more solitude you will gain, as you will be moving further and further away from civilization into more remote areas, complete with panoramic coastal views.

If you hike far enough (about a mile) you will first come to a brackish, yet mostly freshwater pond, marked by a single palm tree in the lava, near the trail. This is a great place to jump in and cool off.

Continuing past the pond, you will soon arrive at a private home, and continuing past the house you will round Weliweli Point and find yourself at Pueo Bay, which affords nice swimming on calm days.

Continuing on still, you will come to a fenced off private area surrounded with a multitude of palm trees - a little oasis unto itself - but strictly off limits to the public.

It was once the property of Francis I'i Brown, a loved and respected Hawaiian businessman and sportsman, but since becoming a historical landmark, in August 1986, it does not give one a welcome feeling, in fact quiet the opposite.

If you continue to hike south farther yet, you will eventually come to Kiholo Bay. Then the trail continues on to Makalewena beach (and this segment of the trail) comes to stop just north of Kona airport.

If you go north, you begin walking along the shore for several blocks length. Where the sand subsides, and just past the Kahapapa Fishpond, the trail becomes very obvious.

There are condos and apartments to your right as you hike. The trail then moves into a more natural setting with trees and vegetation, and then along a ribbon of sand until you reach Anaehoomalu Point. This hike is both pleasurable, and moderately easy with some excellent coastal views along the way.

Soon after you reach the Hilton Resort, the trail turns into sidewalk. The trail does continue past the Hilton and another 9 miles north to Spencer beach, but you'll need strong footwear if you go beyond the Hilton, as there are areas along the trail that include patches of very rough lava.

*The best time to be there: About 45 mins. before the sunset, if your interested in catching the sunset colors and reflections. If you catch the sunset just right, it can be an inspiring experience of a lifetime. You can, of course, access this area at any time, but it can get crowded mid-day to around 6 pm.*

*If your hiking north or south, anytime is good, as very few people take the time to explore these remote trails*

# How to get to 'Anaeho'omalu Bay

Continuing north on highway 19, to the Kona side of mile marker 76, there is a stoplight. It is the first stoplight you come to after the Kona airport. It is Waikoloa Beach Road and here you will turn left towards the ocean.

Just drive straight down Waikoloa Beach Road. You will soon come to a stop sign. There are the Queen Shops to your left. Continue straight another block to the second stop sign. Right after this stop sign there is a Shell gas station and the King Shops on your right.

Continue half a block further to the third stop sign. Here you will turn left. Stay on this road several blocks length and then it will "J" to the right into a big parking area. Park and continue walking on the road, right past the restrooms to the coastline. For those wanting to visit the pond in the foreground, there is a path off to the right, just past the restrooms.

From Kona: Approx. 25 miles
Time from Kona: 30 minutes

# Puako Petrogylph
## Archaeological Preserve

This is a day hike that will lead you to the Puako Petrogylph Archaeological Preserve - for those interested in viewing ancient Hawaiian rock art and learning something about Hawaiian history.

Ki'i pohaku (stone art or images in stone) are what Hawaiians called their petroglyphs. Most petroglyphs in the Hawaiian Islands are found in ancient lava fields, on broad expanses of smooth pahoehoe lava (one of two types of lava, the other being very rough a'a lava).

Of the 150 known Hawaiian petroglyph sites most are located on the Big Island.

Other petroglyphs scattered throughout the island chain, can be found on rocks, cliff faces, in lava tubes, coastal caves, and near or in tide pools.

The majority of ki'i' pohaku were created 1000 to 1,500 years prior to the Western culture's arrival in the late 1700s.

Because of this, these ki'i pohaku are delicate and irreplaceable, so while visiting these sites, be sure to be respectful and stay on designated viewing platforms and paths.

Take care to tread lightly around the ki'I fields, it is forbidden to touch the rock images, walk on them or attempt to make rubbings or casting of any kind, such actions like this can destroy works that have endured for centuries.

The Puako Petrogylph Archaeological Preserve: A shelf

of pahoehoe lava rock about the size of a football field, is hidden in a tangle of forest, where early Hawaiian artists carved an array of arresting figures, some 3,000 strong.

These petroglyphs served many functions: as a historical record, as a repository of sacred legend, and simply as beautiful art.

Once there, you won't be allowed to walk on the fragile lava rock, but circle around the railing and discover individual figures, dancers and paddlers, fishermen and chiefs, hundreds of marchers all in a row, and many family groups.

## Ki'i Pohaku

### Puako Petrogylph Archaeological Preserve

The theme for this highly concentrated field is devoted primarily to rock drawings depicting procreation and 'ohana (family) life.

Continue looking and you will see images from early

ancient Hawaiian daily life everywhere: fish hooks, spears, poi pounders, outrigger canoes, sails, as well as dogs, chickens, turtles, and deity symbols.

*The best time to be there: Early morning and late afternoon, due to the heat of the mid day, otherwise you can access this area at any time.*

## To get to the Puako Petroglyphs

The field of petroglyphs can be accessed from the Holoholokai Beach park near the Mauna Lani Resort. The Mauna Lani Resort is located about 30 miles north of Keahole (Kona) airport.

Turn makai (toward the ocean) into the resort, between mm 74 & 73, go about half mile to a roundabout. Turning right at the roundabout, continue until you reach the Mauna Lani Resort (about a mile).

Just before you enter the resort property there is a sign on the right hand side for Holoholokai Beach park. Park in the parking lot. The trailhead to the petroglyphs is found next to the parking lot.

It takes about half an hour to hike the winding trail through the sparse trees that sprung up on this hardened lava flow. For safety, wear sturdy shoes, and bring plenty of water, as hiking the trail can be very, very dry, and most often hot.

As you hike to the petroglyphs field, keep your eye out for a little cave to your right. You can crawl inside if you wish. Also, take note of some of the petroglyphs that surround the cave.

Shortly after passing the cave, you will come to an

intersection. Go straight to continue to the petroglyph field. Once there, you'll be amazed by the sheer number of petroglyphs.

From Kona: Approx. 28 miles
Time from Kona: about 30 - 35 minutes.

# Lapakahi State Historical Park

Lapakahi State Historical Park provides a scenic walkabout, near and along the Kohala coast, and an educational day hike for those interested in early Hawaiian history and lifestyle.

Lapakahi State Historical Park is the remains an Ancient Hawaiian fishing village. The area was first settled around 600 years ago in the 1300's. Some of the village has been partially restored but most of the rocky walls and remains are original.

This area was rich in natural marine resources for the settlers. But life here was also difficult as the ground is rocky and the area is often very windy.

From the village, you can see miles out to sea. The villagers would watch for the signs of nature to tell them when to fish, when to plant, and when to pray.

Ancient gods and goddesses were the religious backbone of this community. There are a number of heiau (Hawaiian Tenples) located here and a fishing shrine.

Fishing shrines like this one were dedicated to the fishing god, Ku'ula, who lived in the stone. A portion of every catch was left at the stone in return for the god's blessings.

It is hard to imagine living and working in this rugged coastal area. The soil is dry and rocky, and the ocean is often rough and unforgiving.

But generation after generation cultivated and fished and made this area their home. It is a true testament to the perseverance of the human spirit.

The village spreads all along the coastline for miles.
Only a small portion of it has been excavated and
restored for visitors to view.

Pick up a brochure at the visitor center and walk the 45
minute, very interesting, self - guided tour. It will lead
you through several acres of this historical site. Plenty
of water and a having a hat, are a very good idea for
this hike.

As you walk, imagine the sense of harmony necessary
to make life possible here. And feel the peacefulness
that pervades the landscape/seascape.

The village overlooks the protected waters of a marine
conservation area. Easy ocean access and natural coves
made this area ideal for a settlement providing
the mainstay of life for the ancient Hawaiians.

**Along the Trail at Lapakahi Fishing Village**

*The best time to be there:* *Morning is the best time, due to the warm temperatures of the afternoon. Remember access is restricted here and you only have entry from 8 – 4 pm*

## How to get to Lapakahi State Historical Park

From Kona, head north 33 miles on Highway 19 until you reach a tee – the junction of Highway 19 and Highway 270.

At the tee turn left onto Highway 270. A couple of miles along Highway 270 makes a right hand turn, continue on until you see the signed entrance near mm 14 for **Lapakahi State Historical Park** on the makai side (ocean.)

It is open daily from 8 am – 4 pm

(808) 889-7133

From Kona: Approx. 45 miles
Time from Kona: about 45 - 50 minutes.

**Kohala Coast View**
near Mahukona Beack Park

# Mahukona Beach Park Stroll

## Kohala Coast

There is an easy and lovely coastal stroll along a remote part of the beautiful Kohala Coast. It follows the pathway of an old railroad (the rails have long been removed.)

It starts out next to a big tree, and a dirt gravel parking area (see below.) You can easily walk the mile and a half north to Kapa'a Beach Park, but if you do not want to hike that far, hike at least about half way, until you reach where the cliffs has been cut to allow for the train pathway.

You'll know you are there because the wind creates a wind tunnel effect. If it's a bit windy to begin with - it will blow your hat off.

Just before you get there, you will see a sign indicating a Hawaiian sacred site on the right. It is located on the bluff overlooking the sea. It is an ancient voyaging and navigational heiau (Hawaiian Temple) and is known as Ko'a heiau holo moana.

It is the only heiau of its kind in the Hawaiian islands. Ko'a Holo Moana, sometimes called the "Stonehenge of the Islands" consists of a set of standing stones that led the way for ancient Polynesian sea voyagers.

The upright stones are aligned to point specifically to all the neighboring Hawaiian islands, as well as Tahiti, the Marquesas, and other Polynesian islands This is a spot for contemplation and awe, **but be respectful and do not walk within the heiau precincts.**

*The best time to be there: Anytime of day will serve you well along this trail. Sunset will afford you a potential spectacular view, and you can often see whales from late*

*November to late April especially along this coast.*

## How to get to the Mahukona Beach Park Stroll

From Kona, stay on Highway 19, heading north, till you come to a tee. This is near mile marker 67 or 33 miles north of Kona. Here you will turn left onto Highway 270 (reset your mileage gauge at the tee.)

Go approximately 2 miles to the Kawaihae harbor/highway 270 junction. Highway 270 veers off to the right at the junction, **be sure to veer right and stay on Highway 270**.

From the Akoni Pule Highway (Highway 270) you will see the Mahukona Beach Park sign between mm 14 & 15. Turn makai (towards the ocean) here.

Take the paved road down until you reach a bridge, with a big tree next to it, on the right hand side. You will see a little dirt pull over area, and a dirt road that begins there. Simply follow the road, soon you have excellent coastal views and as you continue on - coastal views in both directions.

Once past the wind tunnel area you will be walking through dry grass and a lightly forested area sans any coastal views the rest of the way to Kapa'a Beach Park. The solitude is just wonderful!

From Kona: Approx. 45 miles
Time from Kona: about 45 - 50 minutes.

# Pololu Valley Overlook & Hike

Pololu Valley Overlook is one of the most outstanding viewpoints on the island. You will find it at the very end of highway 270.

This scenic overlook at 400 ft. elevation offers a unique perspective of the rugged beauty of the Big Island, with a view of a fabulous coastline, and a black sand beach.

*The hike down into Pololu Valley is a not to be missed adventure.* Take your time hiking down into the valley, savor the many views along the trail. Spend some time at the magnificent black sand beach. The beach is not a safe place to swim but the whole area is uniquely picturesque.

Walk along the shore to the far side of Pololu Valley. If you want further adventure, there you will find the trail continues up and over the next ridge to the beautiful and secluded Honokane Nui Valley.

The trail into Pololu Valley is located at the end of the Pololu Valley Overlook parking lot.

***The best time to be there:*** *Any time of day is a great time to visit. If you get there at dawn you might be lucky and see cloud colored reflections on the ocean. The same goes for sunset, but just being there any time of day – can lead to a wondrous and uplifting experience.*

## How to get to Pololu Valley

From Kona, stay on Highway 19, heading north, till you come to a tee. This is near mile marker 67 or 33 miles north of Kona. Here you will turn left onto Highway

270 (reset your mileage gauge at the tee.)

**View from Pololu Valley Overlook**

Go approximately 2 miles to the Kawaihae harbor/highway 270 junction. Highway 270 veers off to the right at the junction, **be sure to veer right and stay on Highway 270.**

Simply continue on highway 270 for 28 more miles from the tee, to where the road ends at small parking area. *Take your time here and fully enjoy the experience.*

From Kona: 61 miles
Time from Kona: approx. 90 mins.

View from Waipio Valley Overlook

# Waipio Valley & Overlook

Be prepared for another outstanding vista.
The Waipio Valley Overlook, along with the Pololu
Valley Overlook both offer some of the most awesome
views on the island.

The Waipio Valley Overlook, several 100 ft. above sea
level, and the Pololu Valley Overlook are a great place
to capture an exceptional photo. So don't forget your
camera.

You will need a 4-wheel drive to get in the valley, or if
you just want a vigorous hike to a magnificent location,
definitely opt to visit Waipio Black Sand Beach and/or
explore Waipio Valley.

From the Waipio Valley parking lot, the road continues
downhill on the left, it hits a tee in a short blocks
distance, where you will turn right, and then its down
hill all the way with exceptional views all round.

Just before the road flattens out at the bottom of the
paved, very steep and narrow grade, there is an obvious
right hand turn. To get to the beach, turn right here and
stay on the bumpy, pot-holed, sometimes very muddy
road access. The beach is in about a mile.

Certainly go as far as the river. If your more
adventurous, cross the river (watch where and how
others are crossing it safely.) On the far side of the
beach, on the valley wall, you will see a zig-zag trail
heading up and out the other side of the valley.

This is the 9 mile Muliwai trail that will get you to the
wild and majestic Waimanu Valley. You will need a
camping permit, if you plan to go there.

Otherwise, Waipio Black Sand Beach is an idyllic place to spend the day.

**Wapio Valley River Reflection**

For those wanting to go into Waipio Valley itself, do not turn right on the beach road. Continue straight and in short order the road soon flattens outs and curves left.

Just follow the road as it makes it way through the valley. In about 2 blocks distance you will see spectacular 1,450 ft. Hi'ilawi Falls. When you reach the first *big* stream crossing, where the road drastically dips, you can hike up this stream to the falls.

Thou be forewarned, it is a strenuous hike which includes unending boulder hopping, and crossing and swimming, across the stream many times coming and going.

Beyond the first stream you may continue on about another mile until you reach a very obvious second stream with a sign that reads End of County Road.

This is a good place to turn around, as to continue, is to be going across areas of private property. Please be respect while visiting, it is the home to about 70 residence who love both their home and their privacy.

*The best time to be there: Any time of day is a great time to be there. Like Pololu Valley Overlook - if you get there at dawn you may catch cloud colored reflections on the sea, or the bluff lit up by the first rays of sun. But again, being in the magnificence of Waipio Valley any time of day - lends itself to a fabulous experience.*

## How to get there
## From the Pololu Valley Overlook

Leave the Pololu Overlook area returning the way you came until you reach mile marker 21. At mile marker 21, you will turn left (uphill) onto highway 250.

*This is a very scenic route, and well worth the drive, it will take you to higher elevations, with wonderful views, green rolling hills, and potential rainbows.*

Climb uphill approx. 2 miles until you reach a stop sign. Turn right at the stop sign and stay on highway 250 for a little over 17 miles until it meets up with highway 19. Turn left and follow highway 19 into Waimea.

*\* In Waimea you will come to a stoplight. You will turn left at the stoplight and continue on Highway 19 for another 13.5 miles until you reach a signed left hand turn for Waipio Valley.*

*Once you turn, you will drop down a mile or so, until you come to a stop sign. Turn left here (you are now on highway 240) and follow the highway out another 8 miles until it ends at the Waipio Valley Overlook parking area.*

From Pololu Valley Overlook: 59 miles  Time from Pololu Valley Overlook: approx. 1 hr. 30 mins.

## How to get there Directly from Kona

Go to Palani St. on Highway 19, at mile marker 100 in Kona. Turn uphill. This is the beginning of Highway 190, and it is the most direct route to Waimea from Kona.
Stay on Highway 190 until you reach the first stoplight in Waimea. *At the light continue straight on Highway 19 for another 13.5 miles until you reach a signed left hand turn for Waipio Valley.*

*Once you turn, you will drop down a mile or so, until you come to a stop sign. Turn left here (you are now on highway 240) and follow the highway out another 8 miles until it ends at the Waipio Valley Overlook parking area.*

From Kona: 63 miles
Time from Kona: approx. 1hr. 25 mins.

*Please take notice…* Palani St. is where Highway 19 and Highway 11 meet. The 100 mile marker is the beginning of Highway 19 heading north.

If you go south from Palani St., you will be on Highway 11. It's the same road just with a different starting and/or ending point for each highway.

If you go south from Palani St., you will be on Highway 11 and the next mile marker will read mm 122 and diminish every mile until you reach Hilo.

**Hiking in Waipio Valley**

A Glimpse into Kalopa Native Forest

# Kalopa State Park

## Kalopa Native Forest State Park & Recreation Area

Kalopa State Park is a bit of an anomaly.
It is one of the few places on the island that remains largely untouched.

It retains many of the plants and trees that have been here since before man ever arrived on the island. While large tracts of land on the Big Island have been rearranged to suit the needs of man – for agriculture, ranching, building, and the removal of vast quantities of sandalwood trees (for trade with the British and China.) **Kalopa State Park is unique as a remaining lush native forest**.

This 100-acre State Park and Recreation Area is a great place to spend the day or even just an afternoon, if your short on time. If you are seeking solitude you will find it here – especially once you hit one of the many side trails.

Kalopa State Park has an easy loop called the "Nature Trail," with easy hiking and lots of information about the native forest. There are also several other trails that criss-cross throughout the park.

When you enter the park, drive straight through to the end of the road where you will find a parking lot. There you will discover an arboretum. This can be a fun section of the park for you and your family, as it identifies many of the native trees and plants. This is near an information kiosk and the Nature Trail begins right near.

I'o or Hawaiian hawks do live in the area - sometimes nesting in trees within the park. Be sure to keep an eye skyward now and again, to catch a glimpse of these of these majestic birds.

## Trails in Kalopa State Park:

**Nature Trail:** This is the most popular trail in the park. It's an easy hike of about three-quarters of a mile with about twenty numbered stops to learn about the plants and animals in the park. This hike offers a great way to get a feel for a native rainforest, and kids love it too!

Other close by trails include:

**Robusta Lane:** This 0.3 mile trail travels east-west and links the parking area to Gulch Rim Trail.

**Blue Gum Lane:** This 0.5 mile trail also travels east-west and links the Old Jeep Road to the Gulch Rim Trail in the center of the Park.

**Silk Oak Lane:** This 0.4 mile trail parallels the Blue Gum Lane to the south, linking the Old Jeep Road to the Gulch Rim Trail.

**Ironwood Lane:** This is the most southerly in the Park and links the top of the Gulch Rim Trail to the top of the Old Jeep Road. It also intersects the end of the Perimeter Horse Trail.

**Old Jeep Road:** It's hard to tell that this trail was once a road. It runs north-south for a little over a mile through the center of the Park and connects many of the other trails.

**Gulch Rim Trail:** This trail follows deep Kalōpā Gulch on the eastern side of the Park. It connects the end of Rubusta Lane with Ironwood Lane, passing Blue Gum Lane and Silk Oak Lane.

This is a high, cool rainforest, so plan on getting your feet and pants wet as you hike. Also if you plan to camp here come certainly come prepared for rain. You may be lucky and catch a few sunny days, but best to have what you need in case of rain. At over 2,000 feet in elevation, this Park is much cooler than coastal destinations, so you should consider some warmer clothing, as well

Amenities include picnic tables, restrooms, cabin rentals, and drinking water. The cabins fit 8 people and can be rented for $60/night for Hawai'i residents or $90/night for visitors.

Tent camping is also available for $12/night for residents and $18/night for visitors for up to a six-person camping party.

Visit the Hawai'i State Park website for more information on these cabins and tent camping. Make reservations by calling 808-974-6200

**Hours:** Daily During Daylight Hours
**Entrance Fee:** None

*The best time to be there: For hiking purposes, anytime during daylight hours. Late afternoon allows for a nice soft golden light experience if it's a clear day.*

## How to get to: Kalopa State Park
## Directly from Kona

Go to Palani St. on Highway 19, at mile marker 100 in Kona. Turn uphill. This is the beginning of Highway 190, and it is the most direct route to Waimea from Kona.

Stay on Highway 190 for 39 miles until you reach the first stoplight in Waimea. *At the light continue straight on Highway 19 for approximately 17.5 miles until you find the well-marked turn for Kalopa State Park on the mauka (uphill) side of the road between the 39 and 40 mile markers.*

Keep following signs for the park as you drive uphill on paved roads. Enter the park and you will find ample parking near the cabins at the end of the road.

From Kona: 60 miles
Time from Kona: approx. 1hr. 25 mins.

# Waterfalls on the Hamakua Coast

You may have noticed that once you reached a certain point on your way to the Waipio Valley Overlook, (namely Waimea) things all of a sudden changed color and began to look a verdant green and the landscape became filled with more abundant flora and fauna.

This is because you crossed into the "wet" side of the island, (the north and eastside) where the rainfall is abundant – up to 240 inches a year, compared to the dryer west (Kona) side where the average rainfall is 8 - 14 inches a year.

Once you reach the higher elevation near Waimea, the landscape becomes wonderfully green, and generally stays that way through Waimea and down to Waipio Valley, and also along the Hamakua Coast.

The Hamakua Coast is where we are now about to venture, to some of the most beautiful waterfalls on the island, if not the entire state.

There are a multitude of waterfalls on this side of the island, most are difficult to access. Lucky for us, there are a number of excellent and easily accessible waterfalls.

They are by name, Akaka Falls, Onomea Falls, and Rainbow Falls, plus a few others you will see right along the highway.

While accessing some of them does not constitute a bona fide day hike, they are all worthy of mention, and will certainly add to your over-all nature experience while visiting the Big Island.

**Towering 440ft. Akaka Falls**

# Akaka Falls

Akaka Falls is a unique tropical sanctuary unto itself – one of great natural beauty mixed with wild nature, multicolored plants, and colossal trees. Even though you are walking on a paved path, you feel as though you are walking in a very exotic and remote location.

There are giant bamboo, banana plants, wild orchids, and enormous trees with vines wrapped around them like a fresh scene out of Jurassic Park. There are two large waterfalls, Akaka and Kahuna Falls, and two smaller ones with gentle flowing streams.

When you get to the Akaka Falls viewpoint, after about a ¼ mile hike, you are treated to an amazing vista – a 440 ft. waterfall surrounded by multihued greens including draping ferns, vines, and various indigenous trees.

Akaka Falls was recently voted the most favorite waterfall in all of Hawai'i, therefore, making it the most well-known and most popular waterfall in the entire state. And rightly so, it is a beautiful, majestic, and classic Hawai'i waterfall.

While most people just stop by for a quick photo, take the time to walk more of the trail and explore the area. This is a nice option if you're looking for a little more quiet time and a deeper experience.

*The best time to be there: Is between 9 am and 1 pm, if you want to see sunlight and a rainbow at the base of the falls. Otherwise, any time of day is an excellent time to visit.*

# How to get there: From Kona

Akaka Falls State Park is less than half an hour from downtown Hilo, and about two hours from Kona.

From Kona, go to Palani St. on Highway 19, at mile marker 100 in Kona. Turn uphill. This is the beginning of Highway 190, and it is the most direct route to Waimea from Kona.

Stay on Highway 190 for 39 miles until you reach the first stoplight in Waimea. *At the light continue straight on Highway 19 for approx. 43 miles until you reach mm 14.*

Turn off Highway 19 onto Highway 220 between mile markers 13 & 14 near the town of Honomu. Keep following signs for Akaka Falls as you drive uphill.

The three and a half mile road to Akaka Falls passes through Honomu (a great place to get a sandwich, something to drink, and visit the craft shops, and galleries. Especially give the Woodshop Gallery Cafe a try.

The road after Honomu continues uphill through old sugar plantations and eventually comes to an end at a small parking lot – that fills up quickly.

A lot of visitors park on the road just before, and outside, the parking lot. Admission to Akaka Falls State Park is $1 per person, if you park outside the parking lot. Or $5 per car, plus $1 per person if you park in the parking lot.

Park visiting hours: 6 am – 6 pm

From Kona: 86 miles  Time from Kona : approx. 2 hours.
From Hilo: 17 miles  Time from Hilo : approx. 25 mins.

# Onomea Falls

## Hawai'i Tropical Botanical Gardens

Onomea Falls is a beautiful multi-tiered waterfall within the Hawai'i Tropical Botanical Gardens. If you are a waterfall enthusiast, then you will definitely want to include a stop here to capture these incredible falls.

There are over 2,500 exotic marked plants and an astonishing array of tropical flowers (for all you flower aficionados out there) and an incredible view of Onomea Bay.

There is the $15.00 per person entry fee, but really, for all that you will see (and can photograph) it's well worth it, plus you are supporting their efforts towards preservation and education.

*The best time to be there: They open at 9 am and close at 5 pm with 4 pm being the latest you can enter. Usually between 12 noon and 3 pm is the best time to capture these wondrous falls, otherwise any time of day can be a joy and wonder.*

### To get there: From Kona

Follow Highway 190 to Waimea (39 miles) stay on highway 19 along the Hamakua Coast until you pass the 8 mile marker (49 miles from Waimea.)

Look for the blinking yellow light with sign on the right saying "Old Mamalahoa Hwy." Make the next left onto the Scenic Route. About 1.5 miles on the left is the Hawai'i Tropical Botanical Gardens Visitor Center.

Beautiful Onomea Falls

Time from Kona : approx. 2 hours.
From Kona: Approximately 90 miles

The Garden is located about 7 miles north of Hilo. Take Route 19 north. Just after mile marker 7, turn right at the large blue highway sign on the right saying "Scenic Route." About 1.5 miles in on the left is the Hawai'i Tropical Botanical Gardens Visitor Center.

From Hilo: 8.5 miles  Time from Hilo : approx. 15 mins.

**Thundering Rainbow Falls**

# Rainbow Falls

On the northern edge of scenic Hilo town, the gorgeous Waianuenue, commonly known as Rainbow Falls, flows and cascades 100 ft. into a picturesque refreshing pool.

The Hawaiian name Waianuenue, quite literally means "rainbow seen in water," and gets its name from the colorful rainbows that can often be seen in the swirling mist that rises from the river in the early morning light.

The foliage around the basin of the falls is lush, and tropical. It includes mango trees covered with philodendron, African tulip trees, kukui trees (candlenut - the Hawaiian state tree), banana trees and a variety of tropical flowers.

When the rains are heavy, it is an unleashed torrent of raging water. On most days it is an oasis of beauty and serenity. It is a short hike from the parking lot to the viewpoint

***The best time to be there:*** *Although Rainbow Falls is beautiful at all times, be sure to get there early in the morning before the tour buses arrive.*

*This is also the best time to see the rainbows in the waterfall mists. If you time it right, you could have the falls all to yourself.*

## To get there: From Kona

Follow Highway 190 to Waimea (39 miles) stay on highway 19 along the Hamakua Coast until you pass mile marker 3 in Hilo (54 miles from Waimea,) turn mauka (inland, toward the mountain) on Waianuenue Avenue. As you drive up Waianuenue Avenue, you will pass the Hilo Public Library on your right and soon Hilo High School, also on your right.

After you pass the high school, get into the farthest right lane. You will pass through a traffic light intersection. After you pass through the traffic light, the road will start to curve.

Get into the lane farthest to the right. You will pass a baseball park on your right called Carvaleo park. You will now notice signs leading you to the falls. Take a right onto Rainbow Drive. Drive up a couple of blocks and the parking lot to the falls will be to your right.

From Kona: 95 miles
Time from Kona : approx. 2 hrs. 15 minutes

**Tranquil Rainbow Falls**

# Mokuola

## Coconut Island

While accessing Mokuola does not constitute a bona fide day hike, it is worthy of mention, and will certainly add to your over-all experience while on the Big Island.

It can be an excellent place to take a break from your days travel, eat a picnic lunch, or just bask in the warm sun surrounded by the sea.

Mokuola, most commonly known as Coconut Island in Hilo, literally means "island of life." Moku meaning island and ola meaning life. Historically, people came to Mokuola for sanctuary, for healing, and for spring water believed to have healing qualities.

Mokuola was also a pu`uhonua or place of refuge (as is Pu'uhonua o Honaunau – the first place suggested to visit in this book.)

Mokuola and Maka-oku, the area of land opposite the island where the Hilo Hawaiian Hotel now stands, together formed a place of refuge for defeated and/or wounded warriors.

It was a place where natives could "redeem" themselves, as well as for commoners who sought out needed shelter and safety.

## Mokuola (Island of Life) aka Coconut Island

Today, Mokuola is widely used as a family park and is connected to the main island via a footbridge. As you cross over the bridge, be sure to look in the water for the many honu (Hawaiian sea green turtles) that make their home in Hilo Bay.

The island includes a large grassy field, picnic areas, restrooms, and a few tiny sandy beaches. You can enjoy the day picnicking with your family, fishing, swimming, kayaking, or jumping off a 15 ft. tower into the chilly waters!

It's a great location overlooking the water and looking back towards the Hilo shoreline. Especially in the evening, when all the downtown lights reflect in the bay.

You can spend just a few moments there taking a nice walk around, or you can spend most of the day as it's just a great place to relax and just be.

## How to Get to Mokuola

The easiest way to get there is off Highway 11 between mm 1 & 2. At the stoplight, right next to a well-known Hilo landmark – Ken's House of Pancakes, you will turn left onto Banyan Dr. (The Highway turns from Highway 19 to Highway 11 at the corner where Ken's House of Pancakes is located.

If you're coming from the south (Hawai'i Volcanoes National Park direction) you will go straight at the stoplight – either way you will be on Banyan Dr.

Follow the road past the Naniloa, Uncle Billy's, and the Hilo Hawaiian hotels (about ½ a mile.) Turn right after the Hilo Hawaiian Hotel onto Lihiwai St., then another quick right on Kelipio Pl.

The Coconut Island parking lot is now directly in front of you. Park and cross the footbridge onto Mokuola: the Island of Life!

Beautiful Ha'ena Beach aka Shipman's Beach

Nene ( Hawaiian Goose) near Ha'ena Beach

# Ha'ena Beach

## also known as Shipman Beach

Ahhhh, Ha'ena Beach... That's how you'll feel when you get there, after a rough two-mile jaunt with a changing landscape that includes: sunny open lava ground, shady ironwood forest, a tangled jungle of huge trees, epic wild vines, as well as a tall grassy area near the shore.

The last part of the trail is like a scene out of Raiders of the Lost Ark, where you could expect to find Indiana Jones come running out of the jungle, whip in hand. In fact, a part of the last (4th) Indiana Jones movie was filmed in this location.

You may, at times find the trail – thick with sticky mud and huge puddles, depending on how much and how soon it has rained in the area. Therefore the trail can take some navigation skills and a bit of stamina.

All the same Ha'ena Beach is a bit of a hidden treasure, and the two-mile hike is a blessing as it keeps out the crowds.

The sand is fine and mostly white (a rare thing for the east side of the Big Island, but know that the actual sandy beach is very small and narrow.) Fresh water bubbles up from beneath the sea, and swimming is in a protected cove-like area.

A small cold stream runs down from the historic Shipman house bordering the land, and sea turtles often bask in the sun here.

Ha'ena Beach more commonly called Shipman Beach – because W.H. Shipman Ltd. owns the land surrounding it. And within view from the beach are two large homes, a fresh spring fed lake, Nene (Hawaiian Goose) sanctuary and massive grounds and gardens.

One of the homes is a much older original home and the other is more recently built retaining the Hawaiian style.

Those who make the trek out should be prepared to spend the day, simply to enjoy this unique location. Bring plenty of water, some snacks, and basic beach gear.

Always be aware and cautious when swimming in the cove. Although protected, occasionally large waves sweep in and bewilder the unexpecting. The left side of the cove (facing the ocean) has a stronger current.so best to stay to the right or center of the cove.

As mentioned, the beach is surrounded by many, many, acres of the private Shipman Estate, and this trail is the only way to legally access it.

***The best time to be there:*** *Anytime of day is an excellent opportunity to hike this trail and experience this lovely and remote (usually gentle) beach.*

## How to get to Ha'ena/Shipman's Beach

The turnoff road you are looking for to access the beach is located 10 miles southeast of Hilo. From Hilo, take Highway 11 south toward Kea'au. Just before Kea'au, between mm 6 & 7, turn left on Highway 130 toward Pahoa.

Drive towards Pahoa on Highway 130 and just past the 4 mile marker you will see a sign for Kaloli Drive.

Turn left on Kaloli Drive and take it all the way to where it ends at a tee (just over 6 miles), this will take you through the subdivision of Hawaiian Paradise Park.

At the tee, turn left on Beach Road and head all the way to the end (its just a couple of blocks), there you will see a parking lot and the trailhead to the beach. The trailhead is actually quite wide at the start.

Sometimes the gate to the parking lot is locked, if so, just park directly in front of the big boulders in front of the parking lot and remember not to leave anything valuable in the car here.

Hilo: 17 miles  Time from Hilo: approx. 25 mins.

# A Word About...
## the Ever Changing Landscape!

As of this writing, directions to the next four locations will most likely change, as the access to these locations changes. Presently there is a lava flow expected to hit the town of Pahoa and then soon after, cross Highway 130, the main access route into the lower Puna district.

There are currently two alternative roads in place to allow access when the highway gets covered. They are Railroad Ave. and Government Beach Road.

At some point theses two routes are expected to be crossed by lava as well, as the lava flow continues to wind its way to the sea.

When this happens a third alternate route (which is being worked on right now) will be used. This route will take you through Hawai'i Volcanoes National Park.

When you visit these locations, please find the best way to access them at the time you will be enjoying your adventures.

And until Highway 130 or any other routes are no longer accessible, please continue to use the directions given for ease in reaching each of these sites.

# Ka Wai a Pele
## (Green Lake)

Green Lake is a hidden oasis. Known as Ka Wai a Pele - the "Waters of Pele" to the Hawaiians, it lies within an ancient horseshoe shaped crater with a canopy of flowering tropical trees and undulating thick meadows.

It includes a great variety of fruit trees, including: papayas, coconuts, avocados, mangos, breadfruits, and bananas. It is a world of green wonder compared to its immediate lave prone surroundings.

Ka Wai a Pele was also known in ancient times as the "Waters of Kane", or "Pali Uli". It is sacred to all Polynesia and in one oral tradition is considered the Garden of Eden where all mankind was created.

**Peaceful and Refreshing**
**Ka Wai a Pele (Green Lake)**

Once in this natural sanctuary you can easily navigate down the steep trail to the lake. The lakeshore previously terraced and richly planted in taro and bananas by the Hawaiians, is now surrounded by a sunshade of kukui nut trees and bamboo stands.

If you care to swim, the edge has rich slippery soil and there is plant growth here and there in the lake, but don't let that stop you. A plunge into the waters is very cool and refreshing and the water has a wonderful silken feel to it.

Ka Wai a Pele is actually a spring-fed freshwater lake several hundred feet deep, and is one of the most scenic spots in Hawai'i. It is also one of only two natural freshwater lakes on the Big Island, the other being Lake Waiau at 13,020 ft. on the slopes of Mauna Kea (see page 133.)

Visitors can swim in the lake, walk the grounds, and hike up a road on this property for awesome views in all directions, including the coast and an active volcano.

To gain entrance to Ka Wai a Pele, you must call "Smiley" the caretaker, and arrange a time to meet at the gate to be let in.

The phone number is **808 965 - 5500.**

There is now a small fee to enter - $5.00 per person, but this helps support and take care of this gem, and allows for its appropriate stewardship towards keeping this primal wonder untouched by development.

*The best time to be there: Anytime of day is an excellent opportunity to experience this magnificent oasis.*

# How to get to Ka Wai a Pele

From Hilo, take Highway 11 south toward Kea'au. Just before Kea'au, between mm 6 & 7, turn left on Highway 130 toward Pahoa.

Drive to Pahoa (about 10 miles) and pass the first intersection that takes you into Pahoa. At the next intersection, with a traffic light, make a left at the intersection onto Pahoa - Kapoho Road (this is Highway 132).

Follow this road past Lava Tree State Park. Continue on Highway 132 until it intersects Highway 137 at a stop sign.

Rather than go straight across Highway 132 and onto a dirt road, you will turn right on Highway 137. The entrance gate to Ka Wai o Pele is a couple of blocks down the road on the right hand side. The gate is clearly signed.

Hilo: 25 miles  Time from Hilo: approx. 30 mins.

Along the Scenic Puna Coast

# Ahalanui (Warm Ponds) Park

When you're done with your visit to Ka Wai a Pele, continue south (away from Highway 132) down Highway 137 a couple of miles until you reach Ahalanui Park on the left hand side. It is a gathering place, where many partake of the refreshing waters.

Again, although not a bona fide hike, it is certainly worth a stop here to enjoy the warm pond, relax, picnic, and take a break from your journey.

Walk over and past the pond to where the ocean entry is - at sunset to get a powerful, sometimes mystical view of the gorgeous coast line.

Bring along your swim wear and a towel – it's a naturally thermal heated pool fed from underground springs. It is safe, relaxing, and the price is right – it's free.

**Ahalanui**

**Warm Ponds**

*The best time to be there: If you get there early morning you can observe the sun rise and have the place largely to yourself. The full moon is another excellent time. Otherwise anytime of day is great time to soak in these warm waters.*
Hilo: 27 miles  Time from Hilo: approx. 35 mins.

Wild Wave Splashing along the Puna Coast

# Puna Coast/Red Road

## Hiking Opportunities &
## Leisurely Explorations Await!

Along Puna Coast highway 137, locally known as the Red Road, you can access numerous incredible scenic possibilities. Highway 137 follows the wild coastline.

There are places where you can see the ocean as you drive along the coast and there are also places where you can park your car, and hike in - to access the coast. There is much to explore and discover along this beautiful part of the Big Island.

*The best time to be there: If you get there early you will catch the sunrise and sunrise colors. Otherwise anytime of day is an excellent opportunity to experience magnificent waves, scenic coastal views and often, rainbows.*

**How to get there:** Highway 137 is about 24 miles from Hilo. From Hilo, take Highway 11 south toward Kea'au. Just before Kea'au, between mm 6 & 7, turn left on Highway 130 toward Pahoa.

Drive to Pahoa (about 10 miles) staying on highway 130 until you come to the far side of Pahoa. You will come to an intersection, with a traffic light. Make a left turn onto Pahoa - Kapoho Road (this is also Highway 132).

Follow this road past Lava Tree State Park. Continue on Highway 132 until it intersects Highway 137. The highway is unmarked but you will know you are there when you come to a stop sign. Turn right here, this is Highway 137 and it continues for another 14 miles where it reconnects with highway 130 which will get you back to Pahoa and onwards.

To where you will begin on Highway 137. Hilo: 25 miles Time from Hilo: approx. 30 mins.

Places to explore along the Puna Coast include:

**The Ahalanui Warm Ponds area, Pohoiki Bay, in the Isaac Hale Park area, Mackenzie State Park, the coastal area in front of Seaview Estates, Kehena Black Sand Beach, the new Kalapana Black Sand Beach.**

All of the above mentioned places are in order from the starting point of highway 132 and highway 137.

They are all signed and easy to locate except for Kehena Black Sand Beach and the new Kalapana Black Sand Beach. These two are easy to find, just not signed. Kehena Black Sand Beach is located between mile marker 19 and 20. Closer to mm 19. The new Kalapana Black Sand Beach is located at the very end of Highway 137, see next page for directions.

**Dawn, Puna Coast**

# Kalapana New Black Sand Beach
## Also known as Kaimu Black Sand Beach

Kalapana used to be a small fishing village with a world famous black sand beach, nestled in the picturesque Kaimu bay. Lush groves of coconut trees and a serene seaside park lined its shore.

For many years, surfers and tourists flocked to Kaimu beach to enjoy the high surfs and the incredible fine black sands.

In 1990, lava from Kilauea volcano engulfed Kalapana, as well as the famous black sand beach at Kaimu. The lava flow also destroyed two subdivisions totaling 182 homes, and several miles of public highway.

For several months, the lava continued to flow into the ocean, filling the bay and adding new acres of land to the shoreline.

Now, over twenty four years later, an awe-inspiring phenomenon continues to take place: a new black sand beach is forming where the lava-extended land meets the ocean.

This ongoing transformation is the result of ocean waves crashing relentlessly against the lava shoreline, breaking large chunks of lava smaller and smaller, and then even smaller, into grains of black sand over time.

The young beach not only has a sweeping view of the Puna coastline, but also a stunning volcanic landscape where a looming crater is still active on the mountainside.

## New Kalapana Black Sand Beach
### with Emerging Vibrant Palm Trees

Today with an entirely new coastline and a few poignant traces of the town that once thrived here. A visit to Kalapana is a sobering reminder of the raw power of nature. Standing at this spot, you can't help but feel like you're at the edge of the world!

*The best time to be there: If you get there early you will catch the sunrise. And sunset affords another time of beauty and serenity Otherwise, like the Red Road, anytime of day is an excellent opportunity to experience magnificent waves, scenic coastal views and often, rainbows.*

## How to Get to Kalapana Black Sand Beach

From Hilo take Highway 11 south toward Kea'au. Just before Kea'au, between mm 6 & 7, turn left on Highway 130 toward Pahoa.

Drive to Pahoa (about 10 miles). There you will come to an intersection with the traffic light. At the intersection continue straight through the traffic light - remaining on Highway 130 for an additional 9 miles.

As the road levels off nearing the sea, there will be a left hand turn (just past mm 20) for Kalapana and Kapoho. Turn left here and then a quick right at the tee. Go to the next stop sign (about a block). This is Highway 137.

At this tee, turn right and go a couple more blocks to the end of the road at a big cul-de-sac. Park in the cul-de-sac area and you will see a pathway with yellow painted handrails at the far edge of the cul-de-sac.

This is the beginning of the path that takes you to one of Hawai'i's newest black sand beaches. It is about half a mile walk to the beach.

If you happen to visit on a Wednesday, be sure to pay a visit to Uncle Robert's farmers market. You can't miss it, it begins right there at the edge of the cul-de-sac.

There is live music, wonderful food, excellent crafts, and great people. The market goes from 5 – 9 pm and a fun time is had by all.

Hilo: 27 miles  Time from Hilo: approx. 30 mins.

## Halema'uma'u Crater

### Pluming Halema'uma'u Crater at Dusk

### View from the Jaggar Museum Overlook

# Hawai'i Volcanoes National Park

There are so many wonderful places in Hawai'i Volcanoes National Park, that it would take another entire book to share many of the best locations.

In fact, there is another book available that gives you the best choices and options for day hikes in Hawai'i Volcanoes National Park,

So, let me refer you to another book of mine:

*Day Hikes in Hawai'i Volcanoes National Park: The Best Places to See the Unusual, Find the Unexpected, and Experience the Magnificent!*

If you are going to spent any amount of time in Hawai'i Volcanoes National Park, this is definitely a ***must get*** book. In the meantime let me introduce you to two excellent hikes in the park the Crater Rim Trail and the Pu'u Loa Petroglyph Trail.

But first let me introduce you to Halema'uma'u Crater. Halema'uma'u Crater is one of the crown jewels to visit and experience on the Big Island. Although amazing to experience any time of day, just by its sheer expanse and wonder, the real show begins 40 minutes before dark, regardless of the time of year.

The plume has been a nightly event at Halema'uma'u Crater since March, 2008. A series of earthquakes redistributed the underground lava to the Halema'uma'u Crater to create a lava lake at its base, thus allowing for an incredible and colorful evening plume

Where else do you have such easy access to such a great volcano experience? The Jaggar Museum Overlook is the easiest and safest access to volcano viewing in the world, and awe – inspiring to behold.

## Halema'uma'u Crater with Rainbow
### View from Jaggar Museum Overlook

## The Crater Rim Trail
## What to expect...

This area has landscape and landmark features that are both magnificent and unusual! From the cliff side trail to the striking expansive views from the Steam Vents area - expect to be astonished.

## Halema'uma'u Crater with Ferns
### View from the Kīlauea Overlook Area

This is a fairly easy area to navigate but it may help you to have the **Hawai'i Volcanoes National Park brochure** you picked up at the entry gate. It has an easy to read and understand map, that will visually show you the many trail junctions that are a part of the Crater Rim Trail.

## So let's begin...

**The Crater Rim Trail** loops around the entire Halema'uma'u Crater/Kīlauea Caldera with astonishing views of the crater, as well as vast otherworldly panoramas.

Like a giant hub, there are numerous trails that one can enter and exit upon while hiking the Crater Rim Trail that lead to other fascinating areas and highlights of the park.

As you ring the crater's edge, you will be hiking through various extreme terrains, that includes everything from high desert scrub to beautiful and graceful koa trees, and from steam vents to beautiful ferns and lehua blossoms.

The trail begins at the northern edge of the Jaggar Museum parking lot. It's easy to see, as it has a trail mileage sign, and like several other trails in the park, it's paved.

**Crater Rim Trailhead sign**

This is to allow wheelchair access.
The paved part of the path extends for 1.2 miles, and takes you mostly along the crater's rim.

Once you begin the Crater Rim Trail, you will delight and marvel at the views all around you. Soon you will reach the Kīlauea Overlook (0.6 miles from the starting point.) The Kīlauea Overlook is another fabulous viewpoint.

From there you can follow the edge of the crater in either direction, returning

to where you started, or continuing along the edge of the crater to a number of excellent crater viewpoints, or, to the Kilauea Military Camp - which is where the paved part of the path ends. The full length of the paved trail is about 1.2 miles.

At the Kīlauea Overlook you can also opt to take a short paved trail to the Kīlauea Overlook parking area, where you will find

**Along the Crater Rim Trail**
**Kīlauea Overlook Area**

restrooms, and about a block further along, covered picnic tables (excellent for a picnic lunch in inclement weather.)

**At one point, as you near the Kilauea Military Camp, you will see a very obvious dirt trail off to the right. If you do not need wheelchair access, this is the route you want.**

If you turn onto the dirt trail, you will continue along the crater's edge (with another outstanding viewpoint) where you will soon meet a junction where the Crater Rim Trail will take you to the right.

As the trail begins to descend a bit, you will be hiking through a beautiful koa tree area, with views of the crater off to your right. There are several more viewpoints as you journey forth and make your way to the Steam Vents area just 0.6 of a mile ahead.

**View from the Steam Vents Overlook**

***The best time to be there:*** *Sunset is the best time to watch the glow, get there about 40 minutes before sunset to watch the evening panorama. Another great time to visit is around the full moon, this adds yet another beautiful, if not mystical quality to our experience. Otherwise hiking the Crater Rim Trail can be magnificent at anytime of day*

## How to Get There: Jaggar Museum and the Crater Rim Trailhead

Hawai'i Volcanoes National Park is 28 miles from Hilo. From Hilo, take Highway 11 south toward Kea'au. Once in Kea'au, stay on Highway 11 another 21 miles. The entrance to the national park is clearly marked between mile marker 28 and 29.

From the entry gate proceed straight for 2.6 miles on Crater Rim Drive, you will shortly pass the visitors center on the right (in about a block) a great place for information, restrooms, and free compelling films of the actual lava flows in the park, and beyond.

On the left - across from the Visitors Center, is Volcano House - a historic old hotel on the crater's rim. A great place for a meal, or a snack. It has an excellent gift shop, and fabulous views of the crater, where you can simply relax and / or dine.

Continuing on from the Volcano House / visitor center, you will come to the Steam Vents area (definitely worth a visit.) Then drive past the Kilauea Military Camp, which will be on the right hand side. Here you will find a store, a cafeteria, and a gas station. However, you must be active or retired military personnel to use these facilities.

Continue on another 1.4 miles to the Jaggar Museum parking lot. Park and walk over to the Jaggar Museum. If you make it to the Jaggar Museum Overlook area between 8:30 am and 7:30 pm, you will be able to visit the Jaggar Museum and Gift shop.

### (808) 985 - 6051

The Jaggar Museum is rich with invaluable information regarding the history, geography, and Hawaiian cultural practices in the park. This area also includes a drinking fountain and restrooms.

# Pertinent information regarding your visit to Hawai'i Volcanoes National Park

Hawai'i Volcanoes National Park has the only rainforest in the U.S. National Park system and it's the only park that's home to an active volcano.

It has been designated both an International Biosphere Reserve because of its scenic and scientific values, and a World Heritage Site – for its outstanding natural, historical, and cultural values.

## Visitor Center & Information

Contact info: Hawai'i Volcanoes National Park, P.O. Box 52, Hawaii National Park, HI 96718

www.nps.gov/havo

**(808) 985 - 6000**

The Kilauea Visitor Center is at the entrance to the park, just off Hwy. 11. It is open daily from 7:45 am to 5 pm.

## Eruption Updates

You can also get the latest on volcanic activity in the park by calling the park's 24-hour hot line -
**(808) 985-6000**

Hilo: 28 miles  Time from Hilo: approx. 35 to 40 mins.

# Pu'u Loa Petroglyphs
## An Ancient Hawaiian Trail

The largest field of ki'i pohaku (stone art or images in stone) in the entire state of Hawai'i is at the Pu'u Loa Petroglyphs Preserve within the boundaries of Hawai'i Volcanoes National Park. Pu'u Loa means the "long hill" or "hill-of-long-life" and this area is very sacred to the Hawaiian people.

These ki'i pohaku/petroglyphs here - number well over 23,000, and are dated back between 1200 - 1450 AD. Yes, that's correct over 23,000, ki'i pohaku.

Located on broad expanses of smooth pahoehoe (a smooth type of lava) this vast collection of petroglyphs from the pre and post-contact era, sits right beside a major ancient Hawaiian trail.

While the trail to the petroglyph field is only 0.7 miles long. The trail extends way beyond the ki'i pohaku boardwalk. It continues also, in the opposite direction – directly across the Chain of Craters road (where most people park their car) and then continues on to encircle the entire island.

There were once numerous villages all along the coast that these trails led to… and while the trails remain, all the villages are now gone, due to perpetual lava flows, earthquakes, and tsunamis.

The trail to the ki'i pohaku is easy to follow but is across a rolling lava field so best to wear sturdy hiking shoes and walk carefully as the trail is uneven. There are no bathrooms or other facilities in the immediate area.

It is wise to have water, a sun hat, and a few snacks. It can be pretty warm and dry at times, and sometimes very windy. Occasionally a light rain will fall, but this can be a wonderfully refreshing experience, and if you are really lucky, a magnificent rainbow may appear.

**Pu'u Loa Petroglyph Field**

Once you reach the end of this section of trail (about a 20 minute walk) you will find a wooden

boardwalk raised above the petroglyphs and providing easy views, both of the ki'i pohaku and the immense sweeping landscape.

The hills and swales of pahoehoe surrounding the boardwalk contain thousands more ki'i pohaku, and due to their fragility, Hawai'i Volcanoes National Park advises one to remain on the boardwalk.

Should you feel called to go beyond the boardwalk, be very careful not to step on the petroglyphs as this will

cause the edges to crumble and wear.
Moreover, please be mindful (again, a reminder) that
this *is* a very sacred area to the Hawaiians and one
should treat it with deepest respect.

## Ki'i Pohaku at Pu'u Loa 1

Amongst the ki'i pohaku here, you will find a variety of
human forms as well as simple dots (holes) or dots
surrounded by many shapes -circles, spirals, etc.

You can also find other unique ki'i pohaku, including
fish, starfish, honu, hooks, insects, capes, the moon,
ships, and much more.

The best time to visit the ki'i pohaku is when the
crowds are less, usually this means early morning or
early evening.

One of my favorite adventures here is to go in the early

**Ki'i Pohaku at Pu'u Loa 2**

evening, and stay out through sunset into full darkness around a full moon. Then hike out under the light of a big moon. Once, while walking back with a big moon, it started to sprinkle and I was blessed by a beautiful moonbow appearing on the horizon.

Even with the wind blowing there is a stillness here, a quietude that allows you to immediately go deep within. Be open and listen deeply.

## Getting to the Pu'u Loa Petroglyphs

Hawai'i Volcanoes National Park is 28 miles from Hilo. From Hilo, take Highway 11 south toward Kea'au. Once in Kea'au, stay on highway 11 another 21 miles. The entrance to the national park is clearly marked between mile marker 28 and 29.

Enter Hawai'i Volcanoes National Park, go to the left hand kiosk, drive fifty feet past the kiosk, and turn left on Crater Rim Drive. Continue on Crater Rim Drive until the intersection with Chain of the Craters Road.

Turn left on the Chain of the Craters road, continue to mile marker 16.5 and park at the Pu'u Loa Petroglyphs parking area. This parking area is well marked and has an emergency call box.

From the parking area it is a 0.7-mile walk over a gently undulating pahoehoe lava trail to reach the boardwalk at Pu'u Loa. The trailhead is on the left hand side (same side as the emergency telephone).

*The best time to be there: Early morning is a great time to be there, before the crowds arrive. Sunset also is an excellent time. Another great time to visit is around the full moon. Otherwise hiking the Pu'u Loa Trail can be excellent anytime of day.*
Hilo: 45 miles  Time from Hilo: approx. 1 hour

**Honu (Hawaiian Green Sea Turtles)**
**Resting a Punalu'u Beach**

# Punalu'u Black Sand Beach
## and the Ala Kahakai Trail

There is something different about the Punalu'u Black Sand Beach area located on the rugged Ka'ū coast. Within its remarkable beauty and pervading peace, you will find a unique setting that includes: Hawaiian green sea turtles, a black sand beach, gently swaying palms, incredible wave action, and a fresh water pond... complete with classic purple water lilies.

This is definitely a place you won't want to miss, so be sure to include this scenic site in your itinerary.

Just to the north of Punalu'u Beach is a trail. This is the ala kahakai, or "trail by the sea". It part of an ancient around the island trail that once served as an important link between ritual centers and coastal communities.

Walking the trail, you will find it is still paved in some sections with smooth water worn stones. If you walk north about half a mile on the trail, it leads to a coastal point with interesting viewpoints, and allows for wonderful solitude, as this area is seldom visited.

Spend some time here at Punalu'u Black Sand Beach – hours, or a day if possible. Walk along the coastal trail near Punalu'u Beach and bathe in its vastness and wonder.

*The best time to be there: Early morning is a great time to be there, before the crowds arrive. Sunset also is an excellent time. Another great time to visit is around the full moon. Otherwise visiting Punalu'u Black Sand Beach and/or hiking the Ala Kahakai Coastal Trail can prove to be excellent experience anytime of day.*

**The Ala Kahakai, or Trail by the Sea**
**Just north of Punalu'u Beach**

**How to get there:** Punalu'u Black Sand Beach
and the Ala Kahakai Trail

Punalu'u Black Sand Beach is 56 miles from Hilo. From
Hilo, take Highway 11 south to Kea'au. Once in Kea'au,
stay on Highway 11. You will drive past the entrance of
Hawai'i Volcanoes National Park after mm 28. Continue
on Highway 11 until you come to the 55 mile marker.

Shortly after, you will see the Punalu'u Park sign on the
right. Make the next left hand turn shortly after the
Punalu'u Park sign.

Drive down the hill (a little over a mile) until you come
to where the road levels out and you see an obvious left
hand turn where a number of other cars are parked.
Pull in, park and take it all in (this is an unpaved
parking area.)

There is a small hut on the beach that sells water, soda,
coffee, occasionally foodstuffs (don't depend on the
foodstuffs) and gifts.

Just in case, be sure to have water with you, as it is often
warm, and snacks are always a good idea to have with
you as well, as there is little to nothing in the way of
food choices.

Available services on the northern side of the beach
include drinking water, picnic tables, restrooms,
pavilions with electrical outlets, and camping by
permit.

Once in the Punalu'u Beach parking lot, the easiest
way to get to Ala Kahakai Trail is to face the ocean.
Then head left across the black sand beach with palm

trees, between the ocean and the pond.

At the end of the beach, you will come to another parking lot. Follow the edge of the parking lot along the sea until it meets an old concrete foundation.

Take a couple of steps up onto the foundation and immediately begin glancing to the left. Not too far from the foundation's edge you should notice a trail heading up the face of a bluff.

Climb up the trail and you will be on the *ala kahakai*. Continue forth and you will see the well-worn smooth stones on the trail.

Explore the trail and the immediate area, it is a lovely and remote location, with many fine views of both the sea and the mountains.

Hilo: 56 miles  Time from Hilo: 1 hour, 5 mins.

**Fresh Water Pond at Punalu'u Black Sand Beach**

# La Kae (South Point)
## and Green Sands Beach

South Point is like no other place on the Big Island!
It is often dry and warm, the hills are rolling and
usually golden due to a lack of rain. The wind blows so
consistently that trees grow sideways close to the point.
South Point is a landmass surrounded by the ocean that
is the southern most point in the USA.

Getting there is easy, follow the paved road down from
Highway 11 (about 12 miles, see below) to where it
comes to a fork. At the fork turn right and go about a
mile until the pavement ends.

If you turn left at the fork, this will get you to Green
Sands Beach, more on that momentarily.

When you reach the end of the pavement, park and
drop down to the right where there is a wooden boat
hoist and where most of the people visiting South Point
congregate.

Walk over to the boat hoist and you will find some
exceptional views of the coastline. Be sure to walk to the
edge of the cliffs, and peer down into the amazingly
clear blue water.

There is usually a lot going on in this area, people
jumping off the 40 ft. lava cliff, as well as people
jumping down an old lava tube hole about 40 yards
away from the cliffs that drops into a short sea cave,
you will see local fisherman and other island visitors
enjoying the area. And there is much to enjoy! Just don't
go mistaking this area for the actually Southern most
point.

**Jumping for Joy 1  South Point**

The true South Point – the most southern point in the USA can be readily found, as it is near a 25 ft. high navigation lighthouse tower - that is easily seen from the diving cliffs, boat hoists, and the unpaved parking area where most people gather.

You will want to take the short hike to the navigation lighthouse tower where you will find many fine views in all directions. Once there you may notice a well-worn pathway to the north. If you follow it, it will take you to a large stone with a hole "drilled" through it.

These stones, or mooring rocks, were created to allow for safe fishing from a canoe. A line was tied from the stones to the canoes and the fisherman could fish without worry of being swept out to sea by the especially strong currents at Ka Lae.

**Close Up of (Drilled) Mooring Rock**

If you continue past the first stone and look closely, you will see many more mooring stones.

From the navigation lighthouse tower, visually follow the coastline back inland toward the mountain, where you will see the 500 ft. Pali o Kulani cliffs.

At the base of the Pali o Kulani cliff is a white sand beach, once the village site of Wai'ahukini, an important fishing village because it was a landing site of canoes for

**Jumping for Joy 2  South Point**

travellers heading north on towards Volcano and Hilo.

And once more… from the navigation lighthouse tower, look east (the opposite direction of the "mooring" rock trail) into the distance and you will see a small knoll by name Pu'u Ali'i.

This is the area known as the Pu'u Ali'i Sand Dune site or the Ali'i burial site. It is said this is the place where many king's bones have been laid to rest. If you follow the coastline to the knoll, you will see a wooden sign at its base with the words Ali'i burial site.

There is a short trail that runs to the top of the knoll. There was once a lele (wooden altar) in place here, but time and the elements have claimed it.

From the top of the knoll you will see a small bay with a white sand beach. This bay is known as Kaulana Bay, and if you walk along the shore to it, you will notice random small deposits of green sand.

If you continue walking about 3/4s of a mile past Kaulana Bay along the shoreline - you will come to a boat launch and a 4 wheel drive road. If you continue another 2.25 miles you will arrive at Pāpakolea beach, more commonly known as Green Sands beach.

Yes, it is really a green sand beach, a beautiful area in a lovely bay (Mahana Bay), where on most days one can safely swim.

## The Road to Green Sand Beach

Now back to that left had turn at the fork, if you turn left, this road will take you to an old unpaved parking lot at the end of the paved road (about a mile.)

If you have a standard car rental it is best to park here. If you have a 4-wheel drive or high clearance vehicle, proceed another ¼ mile down to the boat launch (yes, it's the same boat launch mentioned three paragraphs above.)

At the boat launch, is the beginning of the road to Green Sands Beach, it is 2.25 miles to Green Sands. Facing the boat launch turn left and adventure away.

## Magical Green Sand Beach

Whether driving or hiking it is usually very dry and warm, so have plenty of water with you. Continue on the road(s) until you see a bluff rising in the distance, you cannot miss it. There is a trail that runs down to the beach.

Be sure to take the time to explore the many beautiful areas and scenic views of the South Point area!

*The best time to be there: You can catch both sun rise*

*colors and sun set colors here. So early, just before dawn for a.m. colors and dusk for sunset colors. At these times of day color reflects on the clouds and the sea and creates a world of great beauty and wonder. Otherwise, being at South Point anytime of day can be wondrous event!*

**How to get there:** Coming from either Kona or Hilo you will find a very well marked South Point Road sign on Highway 11. From the highway it is 12 miles to the actual point.

At the road sign you are just over 50 miles and about an hour from Kona, and just over 69 miles and an hour and a half from Hilo.

If you have a 4-wheel drive you can drive out to Greens Sands Beach, otherwise it is a 2.25 mile hike each way. About a mile from the actual point you will come to an obvious junction with a sign saying Green Sand Beach to your left and South Point to your right. Either place you go, enjoy, and prepare to expect the unexpected!

**A Seldom Visited Beach**
near the end of Road to the Sea

# Venturing Along the Ka'ū Coast

There are many places to venture and hike along the Ka'ū Coast, as the *ala kahakai*, or "trail by the sea" (mentioned on page   ) follows the entire western coast of the Ka'ū district.

You can access the *ala kahakai*, via Punalu'u Black Sand Beach, as well as by a number of other ways.

One of these ways is down the **Road to the Sea.** This road begins between mm 79 and 80, north of Oceanview. Here you turn makai (towards the sea.) There is a sign that reads Tiki Mama's at the turn, that lets you know your in the right place.

This is a *very* bumpy seven mile road. Best to have a high clearance vehicle , if not a 4 wheel drive. I have seen regular street cars go down to its end, but there are a couple of *very* sketchy places, and I would not recommend it at all. I certainly would not take my car down it.

Once down by the ocean, there is a small white sand beach, a queens bath, and the *ala kahakai*, (the trail by the sea) which you can take in either direction for as far as you'd like.

Be aware - that there is no distinct or obvious trail, it is simple a matter of following the coastline. If you hike north towards Kona, in about a mile you will come to an old jeep road that will take you about 10 miles along the this rugged coast where it reaches civilization and a paved road at the small fishing village of Miloli'i

Get out, hike several miles in either direction and explore the area, you never know what you might chance upon – I will only leave you with these thoughts - that there is as much solitude as a person could ever want, a grand and wild coast, a few ahu (stone shrines)

and some very special places just waiting to be discovered.

Keep in mind… this is a very dry and desolate part of the island, so please plan accordingly and take plenty of water!

**The Perfect Ending to a Perfect Day**
**Along the Ka'ū Coast**

# Mauna Kea

Mauna Kea is the highest mountain in all of Hawai'i, as well as all of Polynesia. If measured from the sea floor it is considered the highest mountain in the world.

**Mauna Kea
with Mountain Shadow and Full Moon**

For the many views alone it is worth the trip to the top of this mountain, especially at sunset. As the sun sets, you will not only see the sunsets warm colors in the sky, you will see the mountain shadow on the clouds, and if you timed it right, a fantastic moon rise.

Looking west, you will see the sun dropping on the horizon and spreading its last rays as the first stars begin to reveal themselves.

There is a short trail from the observatories, to the actually summit, and this trail is open to all, but it is not without its challenges.

At nearly 14,000 ft. there is 40% less oxygen, so breathing itself can become a bit of a task, especially while exerting oneself climbing to the top. Lightheadedness and disorientation can also be factors, so move with caution and be aware.

Acclimatizing at the 9,000 ft. visitor center is the best solution to circumvent high altitude disorientation *before* going to the summit is the best thing to do (see more about this below.)

The weather conditions and temperature will play strongly into your over all experience as well – it is generally *very* cold once the sun sets, and can be *very* windy as well – a combination which can be very unfriendly at times.

**Stairway to Heaven**

**Trail to Mauna Kea Summit**

It is best to have long pants, jogging pants to put over them, or long johns to put under them. A number of layers, or a heavy coat is recommended, if not necessary. Warm gloves and a beanie are a must, as are sturdy shoes and thick socks. And don't forget water so as not to dehydrate.

*Is it worth it, you may be asking –
definitely so!*

I share all this not to discourage you, but rather so that you will know what to expect and what to bring to be fully prepared for a wondrous and safe experience.

*The best time to be there: To view the mountain shadow arrive about 40 minutes before sunset. Observe as everything begins to shift: clouds, colors, lighting, etc. Also, near full moon is a very good time to be there. Be ready, enjoy, and expect the best!*

## How to get there: Mauna Kea Summit

### From Kona Side:
From Kona, go to Palani St. at mile marker 100 in Kona. Turn uphill. This is the beginning of Highway 190. Take upper Highway 190 (Mamalahoa Highway) to the junction of Saddle Road near mm 13. Turn on Saddle Road, Highway 200 (you can only turn one way) and drive to the 28 mm where you will make a left hand turn on to the Mauna Kea Access Road which takes you to the summit.

**From Hilo Side:** Take Kanoelehua Avenue (highway 11) to Puainako Road, which is a block past Wal-Mart and next to the KTA Supermarket. Take Puainako mauka (towards the mountains.)

Continue on Puainako until it comes to a tee at a stoplight (in about a mile and a half.) At this point Puainako makes a jog to the right.

Make a right hand turn at the light and immediately get in the left lane and turn left onto the new Puainako extension, Highway 200.

Follow the new Puainako extension, and within 4 or 5 miles it becomes Saddle Road. Continue on Saddle Road to the 28 mile marker where you will make a right onto the Mauna Kea access road, which takes you to the summit.

From either side of the island, you will be taking Saddle road, Highway 200, to the Mauna Kea Access road located at mm 28. The road is very well marked. From the Saddle road/Mauna Kea access road junction to the summit - it is 14 and 7/10 miles.

The Ellison Onizuka Mauna Kea Visitor Information Center is six miles from the Saddle road/Mauna Kea Access road junction at the 9,200 ft. elevation level.

The Visitor Center is open from 9 am – 10 pm every day of the year, the restrooms are always open. The Visitor Center often offers programs for viewing the planets and stars via telescopes - in the evening (be sure to check out the rings of Saturn.)

Check their website for availability, www.ifa.hawaii.edu/info/vis/.

**The visitor center is a great place to spend a little time to acclimate before proceeding to higher elevations. Half hour is the prescribed amount of time to acclimate sufficiently.**

There you can find food stuffs, water, and a gift area, you may also choose to watch videos of the observatories in action, or go into the fenced area behind the visitor center and visit the lele (wooden altar) or observe the rare Silversword Fern.

Once you acclimate, exit the visitors center, and continue up the hill which shortly turns into a dirt road. At this point there will be a summit conditions sign. The sign also says 4-wheel drive, but it is only recommended and not required.

The dirt road up to the summit used to be poorly maintained and was often very bumpy and wash boarded. More recently they have been regular with the maintenance of it, and it is now a much smoother drive.

Be especially careful and alert while driving on this road, there are few guardrails and the drop-offs are extremely steep, and there are also a number of blind turns. However, the landscapes are fantastic and the views are utterly breathtaking.

After 5 miles, the dirt road will again become pavement. Continue up towards the summit until you meet a tee. At the tee turn right, you are almost there, just another sharp curve to the left and a steady climb in elevation and viola, you are sitting on top of the world!

Go to the highest point, and from there you will see the trail to the top of Mauna Kea summit (Please be respectful here, Mauna Kea Mountain is considered very sacred to the Hawaiians.)

To get back – follow the road back down from the summit and don't forget to stop at the visitor center on the way through for star-gazing and a nice cup of steaming hot chocolate – you certainly have earned it.

**Lake Waiau Sunset Reflection**

**Lake Waiau - Otherworldly Landscape
with Full Moon Reflection**

# Lake Waiau

Lake Waiau is a beautiful gem perched at 13,020 ft. elevation. It is one of only two fresh water lakes on the Big Island, the other being Green Lake (see page 87) and is one considered of the highest alpine lakes in the USA.

Lake Waiau lies in the center of the Pu'u Waiau cinder cone. This cinder cone last erupted about 65,000 years ago.

Along this one mile trail (each way) you will see pu'us (cinder cones - which includes much red cinder of course) fabulous views, incredible clear blue skies, and unique cloud formations. You will feel you are walking on top of the world.

If you plan your hike just right, several days before the full moon, you can watch the moon rise above the ridge beyond the lake, a stunning experience to behold - with the last rays of the sun making the red pu'us look as though they are lite from within, contrasting the deepest of blue skies, combined with a glorious full moon.

Over all, this is an excellent hike for the fore mentions reasons. It is a unique high elevation hike and like the hike to the summit of Mauna Kea requires awareness and preparation.

To help avoid altitude sickness it is advisable to stop at the Visitors Center at the 9,000 foot level for a minimum of 30 minutes to allow your body to acclimate to the altitude.

Be sure to have plenty of water and the extra layers of clothes mentioned in the Mauna Kea summit trail hike.

Much of this area, including the lake itself, is sacred to the Hawaiians. Please be respectful and stay on the trail. Do not enter the lake or disturb the lake or surrounding area.

*The best time to be there: Anytime of day will bring great views. Sunset is an excellent time to be there as the last of the suns light enhances all the colors greatly.*

*And if you can, watch the moon rise from Lake Waiau and then walk out in the moonlight. If you decide to do this, bring along a flashlight just in case, and have plenty of warm clothes, gloves and a warm cap!*

## How to get to Lake Waiau

To get to Lake Waiau, from either side of the island, come up Saddle Road, Highway 200, to the Mauna Kea Access Road turn off at mm 28 (as described on page 129.)

Go to the Mauna Kea Access Road, turn mauka (towards the mountains) and follow the exact directions given until you reach the T, just below the summit, in **How to get to the Mauna Kea Summit** (don't forget to stop at the visitor center and take the time to acclimate.)

At the T turn left, rather than right) and immediately, after the left turn, there is a gravel parking area to your left. Pull down into this area and park.

The easiest access to begin the trail, is by going back to the road and walking along the roadway, on the right hand side, back the way you came.

Walk until you come upon a wooden information sign about Mauna Kea in general, (about 2 1/2 blocks.) The trail begins at that point and goes off into the distance around the base of a large cinder cone.

From the parking lot, it is one mile hike to the lake. Take the trail about ¾'s of a mile until you meet another very obvious trail, and then hike right at this junction. From here you will see Lake Waiua down below.

Remember all the difficulties, in terms of breathing, lightheadedness and disorientation, as well as wind and cold apply here - just like being on the summit of Mauna Kea (which is only a short distance away.)

This trail, is at high altitude with no shade, and often has snow during the winter, so dress appropriately, carry water, and hike with one or more companions. This will insure the enjoyment of your hiking experience, as well as your over all well-being and safety.

# The End of the Trail...

## There is So Much to See and Do

on the big island, with its many breathtaking and stunning features and it many hiking options. The main thing is to allow yourself an over-all safe and wondrous experience.

I hope you will be able to visit many of the places offered and described in this book and that your experiences will prove both inspiring and memorable.

And I hope you will return to this fabulous place and that I will see out on the trail,

Deepest Aloha,

Robert

## About the Author/Photographer:
## Robert Frutos

Robert is one of Hawai'i's most well-known professional nature photographers & camera artists. Robert is also a professional guide, and internationally recognized author.

Robert, who resides in Volcano village, right outside Hawai'i Volcanoes National Park, has spent untold hours crisscrossing the Big Island - exploring tropical rainforest lushness, vast barren lava fields, viewing Halema'uma'u Crater, hiking the rugged Ka'ū wilderness. As well as, the wild and distinctive Puna coastline, and seeking out the best and most photogenic, grand and intimate photo locations.

Robert's credits include Sierra Club publications and many of the nation's top nature calendar companies. His work has appeared in national magazines including: Sierra Heritage & The Yoga Journal, and his work adorns many a book cover. Robert has served as a featured writer offering both photo techniques and inspiration - for Sierra Heritage and Light of Consciousness Magazine

Robert is the founder
of The Light of Aloha Foundation
which offers powerful techniques and dynamic tools to
help you achieve your dreams, follow your inspiration,
and gain an ever-increasing sense of radiant well-being.

Robert has created a unique body of work woven
together from a broad spectrum of training and varied
experience - a spiritual educator, counselor,
professional nature photographer, internationally
recognized author, kahu (minister), teacher,
presenter and healing practitioner,

as well as being a successful multi-business owner that
includes website design and creation, book publishing:
hardcover, soft cover & ebooks, and a photo tour guide
service as well as a sacred site tour guide service.

Robert possesses great depth and passion that inspire
others to meet challenges, rise above limitations, and
transform one's life - into the Best Life Possible.

Robert offers support, encouragement, comfort, and
assistance through mentoring, educating, intuitive
counseling, and spiritual coaching - allowing you a
fresh perspective (the larger picture) a clear sense of
direction, and greater direct inner alignment.

His accomplishments provide some insight
into his passion, enthusiasm, and creativity. Robert is a
gifted teacher/speaker with a unique ability to easily
share and communicate "how to achieve your life goal"
skills.

He brings the same passion – into sharing the Spirit of
Aloha, and the beauty, wonder and magnificence of the
Hawaiian Islands.

**You can reach Robert at:**

www.hawaiiphototours.org

www.hawaiisacredsitestours.com

www.robertfrutos.com

email: rfphoto3@gmail.com     Phone: 808 345 – 7179

## Other Books by Robert Frutos

Clarity, Inspiration, & Optimum Potential: A Concise Guide for Creating Infinite Possibility in YOUR Life!

In the Pursuit of Excellence: A Concise Guide for Creating Unlimited Possibility in YOUR Life, Business and / or Organization!

Photographing Nature in Hawaii: Capturing the Beauty & Spirit of the Islands,

Hawaii Inspiration Aflame: A Passion for the Magnificence,

With Beauty All Around Me: Inspirations to Touch the Heart, Heal and Uplift the Spirit

Walking in Beauty: Inspirational Seed Thoughts for Creating YOUR Best Life Possible

Light on Hawaii: Capturing the Dynamic Islandscape, A Photographers Approach

Aloha Spirit: The True Essence of Hawaiian Spirituality

for more information about these books, go to:

www.hawaiisacredsitestours.com

Click on Robert's Links / Books

Lastly, I have one more photography book available, an inspiring coffee table book entitled: **Hawaii Inspiration Aflame: A Passion for the Magnificence**, for those who would like to see more extraordinary Hawai'i images, it includes images from some of the other Hawai'i islands as well. This book is available directly from the author and the cost is $65.00, plus shipping. Email me at rfphoto3@gmail.com for more info. or to obtain a copy.

## An Offering to Pele

Made in the USA
Middletown, DE
02 December 2022

15863007R00080